the
Picture Framing
Handbook

the
Picture Framing
Handbook

Andy Parks

WATSON-GUPTILL PUBLICATIONS/NEW YORK

A QUARTO BOOK
Copyright © 2009 Quarto Inc

First published in the United States
in 2009 by Watson-Guptill Publications,
an imprint of the Crown Publishing Group,
a division of Random House, Inc., New York
www.crownpublishing.com
www.watsonguptill.com

Library of Congress Catalog Card Number:
2009920542

ISBN 978-0-8230-9801-9

QUAR.PICF

Conceived, designed, and produced by
Quarto Publishing plc
The Old Brewery
6 Blundell Street
London N7 9BH

Senior editor: Lindsay Kaubi
Art editor and designer: Anna Plucinska
Copy editor: Clare Hubbard
Art director: Caroline Guest
Design assistant: Saffron Stocker
Photographers: Phil Wilkins
Illustrator: William Donohoe
Picture researcher: Sarah Bell
Creative director: Moira Clinch
Publisher: Paul Carslake

Color separation by PICA Digital Pte Ltd,
Singapore

Printed in Singapore by Star Standard
Industries Pte Ltd

10 9 8 7 6 5 4 3 2 1

Contents

Preface

I have been involved with picture framing for twenty four years and have successfully run my own picture framing business for the last three; I also teach picture framing to adults. During my time as a picture framing teacher, I have adopted a clear step-by-step approach; slowly adding each picture framing technique or skill to each student's experience, and ensuring a good result from each stage before moving onto the next. It's my aim to carry this clear step-by-step style into each different technique in this book.

The book begins with an overview of the necessary tools required to frame pictures successfully. This is followed by an exploration of ideas about choosing mats and frames to suit pictures, and highlights the need for careful consideration when choosing picture-framing materials. At the heart of the book are the basic and advanced step-by-step techniques. The techniques covered include mat cutting, frame cutting and assembly, glass cutting, fitting the picture and, finally, hanging the picture on the wall. More advanced techniques include double or slip mats, multiple aperture mats, framing 3-D art and needlework, and framing art on canvas. To enable you to add an individual look to picture frames, a section on frame and mat decoration rounds off the step-by-step sections. As a framer with many years' experience, I recommend that you familiarize yourself with each stage and practice each technique to improve your results.

I believe this book will provide something for everyone, whether you simply want to frame your own artwork or want to take up picture framing more seriously.

Andy Parks

Introduction

There is no such thing as the "right" frame for an artwork. A vast choice is open to the collector, artist, or framer, and in the end the choice of frame is a matter of personal taste, which is why framing is such a fascinating subject.

There are some principles, however, which really need to be followed. Different types of frames should be used for different types of artwork, and a frame should be chosen that enhances the individual characteristics of the artwork. The style and color of the frame and mat should not fight the artwork for attention, nor should they detract from the image.

OILS AND ACRYLICS

Oil and acrylic paints have a texture that makes the painting stand out, especially when the artist has used them in a thick or impasto manner. When framing most oil paintings, therefore, you are dealing with something that is in relief. It is this that governs your choice of frame; it also helps to broaden the choice. You can sometimes make do with narrow frames, such as wooden or metal strips, that do not cover any of the surface of the painting. This is a suitable approach if the painting is strong enough to stand out on its own and a slim boundary will suffice.

On the other hand, a strong painting can also take a strong frame. This is especially useful in the case of a small painting. The presence of a wider frame will help to focus the eye onto the painting itself.

WATERCOLORS

Glass is nearly always used to cover watercolor pictures because they are far less durable than oils or acrylics. Watercolor frames tend to have a subdued look, reflecting the muted tones of the pictures they contain. This framing style is suited to older watercolors but some modern pictures deserve a brighter context.

Watercolors have a fragile appearance, so it is generally not a good idea to surround them with a densely colored mat. This explains why traditional watercolor mats are white, cream, or pastel.

A common characteristic of watercolors is that the paint is rarely taken right up to the edge of the paper. This gives the framer the option of leaving this area showing, and enables the viewer to see how the washes of paint affect the paper.

PHOTOGRAPHS

Old sepia photographs can generally be enhanced by being framed in a traditional style, in keeping with their nostalgic appearance.

Treatment similar to that of a watercolor is usually best for modern photos; use a neutral-colored mat and leave the edge of the photograph visible. Neutral colors for mats work well with modern photographs, but sometimes a contemporary black-and-white image can be set off by a brightly-colored mat. Color photos can be placed in a black-and-white or color setting, provided it repeats a theme present in the photograph.

Modern photos usually look their best in a simple setting—a narrow metallic band or a plain black frame.

Needleworks and 3-D artworks should be framed in deep box frames to protect them.

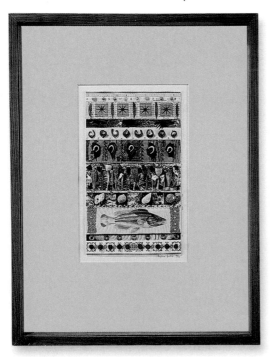

PRINTS

Contemporary prints can be freely interpreted when it comes to choosing a frame. Simple frames, such as those made of colored wood or a metal strip, often look effective.

There is one general rule, which applies to both old and new prints; leave the edge of the print showing. In a good print, this edge should be a crisp line but all edges are interesting because they show how the colors of the print are laid on top of each other, so that they meet in their exact positions in the composition.

NEEDLEWORK

The way to prevent a piece of needlework from becoming tattered or worn is to frame it. Needlework should first be stretched around a board and laced at the back with thread (see page 102). Glass is needed to protect needlework, but avoid placing glass directly onto the surface. An insert or some other means must be used to separate the fabric from the glass pane.

3-D ARTWORKS

Many people like to display 3-D items on the wall. This might be a collection of medals, a collage, beads, or other materials. This calls for a box frame. Box frames are basically an ordinary frame, but with a deeper insert.

Any 3-D item that is likely to gather dust should be placed under glass. Extra care is needed for work of a more enduring nature, such as ceramics, jewelry, and small pieces of sculpture. Such items stand out alone, and often need the simplest of settings.

chapter 1

Tools, workspace, and materials

There are several considerations to take into account before you begin framing your own pictures. First, you will need a number of specific tools to achieve good results, you will also need a workspace suited to framing, and you will need to know how to choose framing materials that complement your pictures. This chapter looks at tools, workspace, and materials, and offers advice on getting started.

Essential tools

All the tools that you will need to complete your picture framing projects are detailed in this section. You will probably want to keep your initial expenditure on tools as low as possible, so the prices of the various items will be discussed. It may well be that you have many of the more basic items in your toolbox already, so check to see what you already possess.

CUTTING MATS

Cutting mats protect the workbench surface, provide a clean surface to work on when you come to fit your pictures, and also keep the blades of cutting tools sharper for longer. Self-healing cutting mats are particularly useful because they are nonslip. An alternative to cutting mats is an old sheet of matboard but this will not preserve the blades of cutting tools for as long as the self-healing mats. Medium-density fiberboard (MDF) or hardboard should not be used because they will create unwanted dust and also blunt your blades very quickly. Each mat type can be secured to your bench with small pieces of adhesive putty to prevent them slipping around.

1. Cutting mat
2. Matboard
3. Matboard
4. Long metal ruler
5. Short metal rulers
6. Pencil
7. Eraser

PENCILS, ERASERS, AND RULERS

A sharp pencil and an eraser will be necessary for all your projects. It is recommended that the pencil has a reasonably hard lead, being #2 or harder. The eraser should be soft with plenty of clean edges, so a new one may be a good idea.

A steel ruler with an undamaged straight edge is an essential tool. Do not use an aluminum straight edge or ruler because it will quickly become uneven with steel cutting knives running along it. Aluminum also dents easily if the ruler is dropped. The ruler should have clear and easy-to-read measurements along it. The ruler should be at least 24 inches (60cm) long. If you intend to frame larger pieces of work regularly it may be prudent to obtain a longer ruler for these projects.

Retractable knife blades

Retractable knife (above) and scalpel (below)

KNIVES

The knife used to cut out mat and backing boards needs to be easy to hold and should always have a sharp blade. Strong retractable knives are recommended for cutting all of the boards used in this book. Retractable knives are usually held together with a screw, and spare blades can be stored inside. Craft knives or scalpels (pictured in red in the photo above) can be used for cutting thinner sheets of board, but these tend to have thinner blades and can snap during cutting.

GLASS CLEANING: CHAMOIS AND COTTON CLOTH

There are many glass cleaners on the market but the cheapest and the most effective is a chamois. Soak the chamois in cold water to make it wet, gently wring out, and clean the glass. Then use a clean, dry cotton cloth to polish the water off the glass. Other glass cleaners can be useful for really dirty glass but these can still smear. Therefore use the glass cleaner to remove the dirty areas and finish off with a wet chamois and then a dry cotton cloth.

Cotton cloth

Chamois

SPONGE AND WATER

These are used for wetting gummed paper to attach pictures to overmats and also to seal the backs of the picture frames. Use a shallow bowl or plastic lid filled with water. The best sponge to use is a slice of a car-cleaning sponge so that it makes a wide face but keep the sponge thin in order to hold as much water as possible on its top side. Keep topping up the water level to ensure that the tape will stick.

HAMMER AND NAILS

For picture framing you should always choose a lightweight tack hammer. If the hammer is too heavy the frames can easily be damaged or split. The nails used in framing are very thin and are called 19-gauge or veneer pins. They are sometimes called panel pins, depending upon where you buy them. The thinner the nail the better because if the nail is too thick it can split the molding. Also, thicker nails are more visible from the side of the frame. The most useful nails are 1 inch (25mm), but longer nails will be needed for larger frames.

BRADAWL

A bradawl is used to make pilot holes for screw rings and D rings for hanging up pictures. Make sure the bradawl has a sharp point, and a good handle for gripping is essential.

MITER SAW

A miter saw is probably the cheapest and one of the more accurate tools for beginners needing to cut picture frames. The miter saw is basically an enhanced hacksaw on a purpose-made housing. The saw also has a measuring system to help with repeat measurements. The saw usually comes with a base plate that can be clamped to a workbench with a G clamp. If you have a bench dedicated to picture framing the saw can be permanently screwed to it, but a temporary G clamp will suffice and this frees up useful space when it is not in use. The blades of the miter saw are easily interchangeable and the preferred blade is a 14 TPI (Teeth Per Inch) blade. There are finer cutting blades available, such as a 24 or even 36 TPI, but the blade that the miter saw is supplied with will usually suffice.

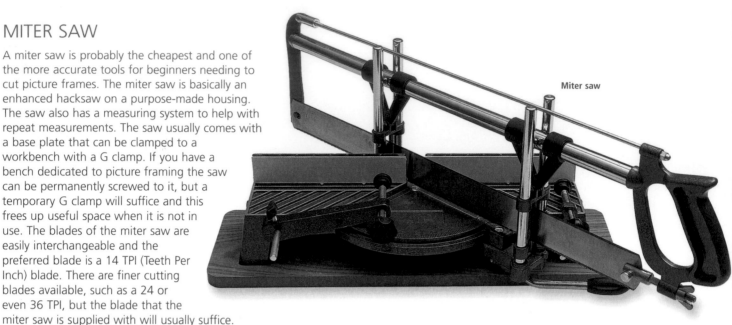

Miter saw

G clamp

Miter vises

MITER VISE

Vises are used to clamp the picture-framing molding together while gluing and nailing the frame corners together. They are available in many sizes and generally the heavier vises made of steel will be stronger and more effective. However, the cheaper and lighter aluminum ones will work just as well on smaller molding widths up to 2 inches (50mm). Try to buy two miter vises because this will help when assembling the frame. The vises can be screwed onto your workbench or onto a piece of wood and clamped to the corner of your bench. Only one should be secured because the second vise's clamping position on the bench will vary for each different size of frame.

UNDERPINNER

Frames can also be joined using wedges (or V nails as they are often called) that are driven into the underside of the frame corner using an underpinner. Underpinners provide an excellent method for joining picture frames but they are generally expensive to buy and take up a lot of space, which could be an issue.

MAT CUTTERS

Mat cutters enable the picture framer to cut an overmat accurately with a 45-degree beveled edge. This beveled edge adds a professional appearance to any picture-framing project and also helps to lead the viewer's eye into the picture.

There are many mat cutters on the market that will cut at 45 degrees. You should make sure that the one you buy has its own straight edge and that the straight edge has a purpose-made groove to ensure the mat cutter does not "wander off" line during the cutting procedure. Most cutters will have both a 45 and a 90 degree cutting blade (sometimes on the same cutting head, sometimes on two separate heads).

There are also much larger machines available for frequent use that have border stops built in so that you do not need to mark out each mat. However, these machines are far more expensive and do take up a lot of space. The difference in quality between the two types of machines, with a little practice, is fairly negligible. Unless you are intending to cut a lot of mats it is best to keep to the smaller, cheaper cutters. You can always invest in a larger machine as your needs require.

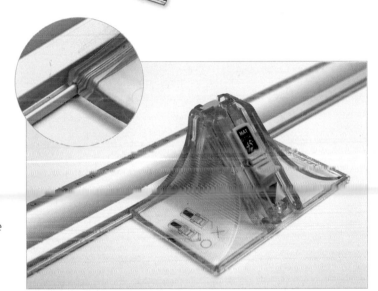

Handheld mat cutter with a straight edge

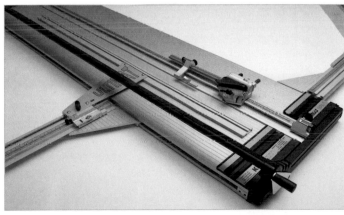

Tabletop mat cutter

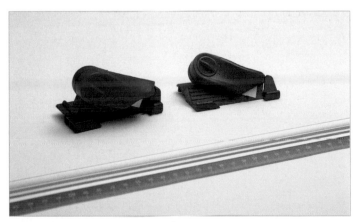

Basic mat cutters

Workspace

Your workspace needs to be considered carefully. Of course, it may be that the only workspace available is the kitchen table, but that isn't a problem. Nor is using the backyard storage shed or garage as a picture-framing workshop. This section gives some helpful hints and key pointers that will assist you in producing a good working environment, wherever it may be.

If possible, have a combination of natural daylight from a window and artificial light. A strip or fluorescent light can help to provide an even light and reduce shadows that can make aligning mats or miters of frames awkward and cause inaccuracies.

A toolbox, or even a tray, is definitely a good idea as the tools will be out of harm's way and it should make it easier to find each item as required.

Ideally, the workbench should be about 34–36 inches (85–90cm) high. This means that the picture-framer's posture is not too stooped and avoids backache. This height will also enable you to sit down to work but the seat will need to be a tall stool.

Small pots and cans or small draw storage systems are a useful way of storing the various fittings. This way they are always ready to hand. Keeping them safely stored away will also reduce the risk of denting the frames or mats (or even damaging the picture) on a stray nail or screw eye.

Try to keep the work area as dust-free as possible. A vacuum cleaner is useful, as is a dustpan and brush, but be careful not to swirl up a lot of dust with a brush before fitting the picture because the resulting airborne dust will appear underneath the glass as if from nowhere.

The workbench should be a perfectly flat surface and covered with cardstock to keep the area clean. When fitting frames an old blanket or sheet can always be used to protect the surface of the frames and prevent scratches.

Make sure the working environment is not too damp. Don't leave matboard in a shed or garage for long periods as it will absorb water like a sponge, which will cause damage to the overmatted picture in the long term.

Make sure that you can walk around at least two sides of the workbench. This is especially useful for larger projects.

Moldings

The molding is the frame itself, the outer edges that most people have in mind when they think of a frame. Molding is available in strips of wood similar to the carved pieces that surround many doors and windows. Picture-frame moldings are available in thousands of different colors, styles, and profiles. This section shows some of the most popular moldings and their uses. It is worth pointing out that the choice of picture-framing materials is subjective; one person's choice may well not be another's. However, there are some basic decisions that can be approached in a systematic way.

Dark wood moldings

Colored moldings with gold inner edge

Colored reverse moldings

Silver profiles

Ready-made framers' moldings are available in huge variety and are to be found in art shops and picture framing suppliers. The choice of picture-frame moldings can seem a little daunting. When presented with a wall or a revolving display full of samples, the immediate question is—which one?

Hundreds of options need to be narrowed down to just one, so do take a little time to consider this important decision. Each picture is only going to be framed once (hopefully!) so make sure the materials that are chosen complement the picture. It does not matter if the picture framer can cut the best overmat, miter and

assemble the best frame, and fit the picture into the frame without leaving any dust or marks behind the glass if the frame color is wrong for the picture.

Molding choices are almost unlimited, but a few basic considerations: suitable colors for the picture, the surrounding décor, size of molding for the picture, and safety with regards to the glass—should narrow down the choice fairly quickly to just a final few before the preferred choice is made.

Stained pine
moldings

Open-grained
profiles

Large, colored
moldings

Colored cushion
profiles

Large profiles

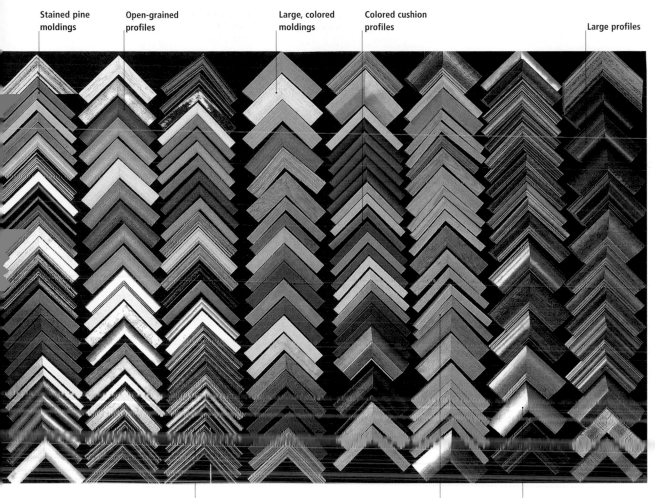

PROFILES
This wall of
molding
samples—
typical of what
would be found
in a framer's
studio—gives
an idea of the
vast range
available.

Colorful gold
moldings

Plain wood
profiles

Large, stained
wood and gold
profiles

Choosing materials

Does the picture framer choose the materials to suit the picture or to match the surrounding décor? It will depend entirely on each individual's choice and perspective. The choice of materials is most likely to incorporate both the picture and the décor of the hanging environment, but not always. Some argue that the frame must suit the picture and ignore the décor, others that a frame must match its surroundings. Only you can decide, but each side of the argument should be considered. However, if in doubt, a good starting point is to ensure that the picture framing materials complement the picture. If this means that the framed picture does not suit the décor, then maybe an alternative hanging place should be found.

SQUARE COLOR PROFILES

CURVED COLOR PROFILES

When first choosing a molding, a simple square profile is a good place to start. This profile is made from pine and is about ¾ inch (19mm) in width. It is one of the easier frames to join because the outer edge is flat. This is an important consideration, especially in terms of nailing the picture frame corners together. The profile is usually available in many different colors, including blacks, grays, and shades of brown.

A slightly wider version of the same square profile is another popular choice. This is also available in many different colors. The slightly wider width of 1¼ inches (30mm) may be preferable for larger pictures but be careful not to overframe any image. This is an easy mistake to make and can have the effect of drowning out the picture.

This range has a slightly curved profile. The colors appear more subtle in this range because the added white wax creates a toned-down color. This profile could present a problem with nailing but a carefully positioned pilot hole should work well.

CLASSIC BLACK PROFILES

PLAIN WOOD PROFILES

The open grain in this range of profiles provides a driftwood effect and, again a reasonable choice of colors is available. Colored frames are very popular when trying to match picture-framing materials with décor.

Classic black moldings are available in many different shapes and sizes. They are also available in matt or gloss finishes. Black frames can create or exaggerate contrast in a picture and are not solely limited for use with black and white pictures. Again, be careful not to draw the viewer's eye away from the picture with too wide a choice of black molding. This molding measures about 2½ inches (62mm) wide and could easily dominate a subtle picture.

Plain wood moldings are popular and are available in many different profiles. Plain wood can be an easier, neutral choice for a frame. This may also be a good choice to complement certain décor. Plain wood frames can be stained or painted for a unique effect. See "Mat and frame decoration" on page 114.

LARGE PROFILES

Larger moldings, such as this broadly curved one, are generally available in fewer choices of finish and will also tend to be more expensive.

Large, elaborately shaped profiles are often available only in gold or silver, and certain profiles, such as this one, may present a challenge if they are to be joined with nails.

This triangular gold molding could look very effective around a mirror.

This large gold molding would suit an old masters oil (the original or a print of the original).

Bigger moldings, like this, should be used on bigger pictures. One of the main reasons for not using a small molding on a large picture with glass is the weight.

Deep rebate or box profiles are very useful for framing 3-D artworks. The added depth can also help to exaggerate the 3-D nature of the picture.

REVERSE PROFILE MOLDINGS

Traditionally, profiles slope in toward the picture, but the profile of a reverse molding slopes away from the inner edge of the frame, so this is the "reverse" of the normal. Reverse profiles can look effective on many kinds of pictures, but they can lead the viewer's eye away from the picture.

A good compromise, if the reverse profile is preferred, is a stepped profile. It is also available in many colors. The range shown above uses mottled gold and silver mixed with reds, blacks, and greens instead of solid colors.

Slip frames

Canvas and gold slip frame

Gold slip frame

THREE FRAMES
This oil painting gains a 3-D effect from its three frames.

The picture framer does not have to stop at one frame. The use of slip frames on the inside of the main frame can add depth to a picture. Slips are traditionally gold or canvas and gold but are becoming increasingly available in many different colors. The slip can also be used to keep glass from touching pictures, such as pastels or charcoals. Gold slip frames are a very traditional method of picture framing and though no longer fashionable are still remarkably effective.

Choosing picture-framing glass

There are several different types of picture-framing glass available and most are approximately ¹⁄₁₆ inch (2mm) thick.

Plain glass is by far the most common kind. However, there are a number of reflection-reducing glasses available. The first choice is diffused or nonreflecting glass. If the picture is going to be hung where there is a lot of light shining directly onto the picture frame this could help make the picture more visible to the viewer. In the photograph, right, the reflection of the direct light on the two glass types is clearly visible on the plain glass on the left. It is not as obvious on the nonreflecting glass on the right.

Nonreflecting glass should only be used when one overmat is used to mat the picture. Any extra distance between the nonreflecting glass and the picture through the use of double or even triple slip mats may make the image impossible to see clearly.

There are more specialized glasses available to the picture framer, such as museum glass. These types of glass are designed to filter out most of the more harmful ultraviolet light that will, in time, damage your pictures and cause them to fade. These glasses are very expensive to buy but they are recommended if you are framing a picture of particular value.

Plastic or acrylic can be used instead of glass where safety issues are a major consideration; if the pictures are to hang in a child's room, for example. Plastic is far easier to cut and safer to handle, and will not shatter if the frame falls off the wall.

Left: plain glass; right: nonreflecting glass.

Mats

A mat provides a border for the picture you are framing, cut with a 45-degree bevel on its inside edge. Mats are made from matboard, a material specially made for the purpose. Matboard can be many different colors but the inner core, revealed by the bevel, is usually white.

The various colors that are available help to complement tones in each different picture that is overmatted. A simple off-white or cream mat is perhaps the most popular choice and represents a neutral choice of materials.

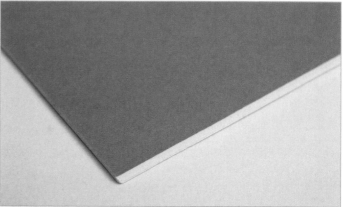

Darker colored matboards can add a more dramatic feel to a picture but can easily dominate as well.

White mats can add contrast to the picture but can also be too light and create a "washed-out" effect.

Mats are not always a smooth, one-color style. This is an example of a flecked mat that could match a style in the picture.

Matboard is usually around 1/16 inch (2mm) thick and is available in sheet sizes up to approximately 64 x 44 inches (1.5 x 1m). There is a vast choice of colors, finishes, and textures available.

The mat can also have a textured effect to the surface paper. This can help to prevent the "washed-out" effect especially on lighter-colored matboards.

Matboards are also available in different levels of conservation quality. This one has what is known as an "acid free" level of conservation and also has a bevel that is the same color as the top surface paper.

Tip

Because one of the main purposes of framing and matting is to preserve the paper inside the frame and mat, paper conservation is an important aspect of picture framing. This is especially important when framing anything of value, whether financial or sentimental. Consult a local picture framer about conservation framing for more advice on choice of materials, but at the very least the matboard used should be of a neutral pH level.

COLOR

Take care when choosing the mat color because the wrong choice can easily spoil a good picture. Take time to consider the various options and, if in doubt, choose a neutral cream mat.

Aesthetic decisions

The choice of picture-framing materials available is vast. This section demonstrates how a picture can be affected by different choices even when the differences between the styles and materials are very subtle.

BORDER WIDTHS

The first aesthetic consideration is the width of the overmat. Unfortunately there is no simple formula for deciding the width of the mat borders for a given size of picture. There are, however, some general rules.

The mat should be wide enough to help lead the viewer's eye into the picture. If the mat is too narrow this effect will not be achieved and the picture may appear "squashed" into the frame.

On the other hand, if the mat is too wide, the picture can become "lost" in the picture frame.

FRAMING A MONOCHROME PICTURE

When framing a simple monochrome picture, such as this charcoal drawing of a horse, there are a series of aesthetic decisions to make, some examples of which are shown below.

The different effects, both on the picture itself, and the overall impression, are clearly visible. Make sure you take a little time to choose your materials carefully to ensure an aesthetically pleasing effect is created.

MAT COLOR

"If in doubt, use a cream mat." The picture is enhanced with a single off-white or cream colored mat. There is a slight contrast with the paper that the charcoal has been sketched on.

A single black mat makes the image appear more dramatic by instantly adding strong contrast between mat and artwork. However, harmony is retained because the black of the mat echoes the black of the charcoal.

A double or slip mat (see page 78) combines the off-white and black mats together. The inner black mat is visible by ¼ inch (6mm) and the outer off-white mat is about 2½ inches (62mm) on the top and sides and ¼ inch (6mm) deeper on the base. This creates a 3-D effect, and focuses the viewer's eye on the horse.

Overmats are often cut with ¼ inch (6mm) more at the base. This is for two reasons. First, the frame is always cut approximately ¹⁄₁₆ inch (2mm) bigger than the overmat. This is to allow for ease of fit and also for the expansion and contraction of materials. With the effect of gravity, the matted picture will sit on the bottom of the frame. When framed, ¹⁄₁₆ inch (2mm) more mat will be visible at the top of the mat than at the bottom. Second, human vision creates the optical illusion that evenly bordered mats have a larger top than base.

This example shows a 10 x 8–inch (254 x 200mm) photograph with a mat border width of 2½ inches (62mm) on each side. The overall effect is balanced and aesthetically pleasing.

Although there's only a slight difference in depth between the two borders, the deeper base on the mat on the right makes the mat appear more balanced to the human eye.

FRAME TYPE

A black and a plain wood frame are added to the single off-white mat. The black frame adds contrast whereas the plain wood frame gives a warmer, softer effect.

A black and a plain wood frame are added to a single black mat. The black frame merges with the black mat but has a "clean" effect. The wood frame seems somewhat fussy next to it.

A black and a plain wood frame are added to a double mat. The black frame echoes the black inner mat and charcoal. The wood frame offers a pleasing contrast to the black inner mat.

MATTING COLOR PICTURES

This 24 x 24–inch (60 x 60cm) oil painting of an acer tree has many bright primary colors and there is no one easy area or color to emphasize or tone down with careful choice of materials.

1	2
3	4

1. Off-white overmat. This is possibly too light in color and does not really enhance the picture, rather it washes it out.

2. A warmer and darker tone of off-white or cream works a little better because the specific tone is present in the picture.

3. Gray overmat. This gray, although it is another neutral, is too cold and does not reflect the temperature of the colors in the picture.

4. A black mat appears heavy and deadens the colors of the painting.

5	6
7	8

5. The picture has many darker tones present so perhaps a darker mat may work? The use of a blue mat echoes the many blue tones present in the painting. However, the cold blue does create a cold overall effect.

6. The warm tones can be emphasized with a warm colored mat. Here, a red mat is used to highlight the fall tones. However, red mats can easily dominate a picture and the eye will be drawn to the mat and not the picture.

7. A warmer tone definitely suits the picture but the red is too strong. This more neutral sand or beige color works well.

8. Green complements some of the colors in the background of the picture. This choice lets the image speak for itself, simply providing a neutral border.

Using a double mat

Creating combinations of colors using double mats can produce markedly different effects to single mats. Generally, the inner mat color choice of ¼ inch (6mm) will emphasize that color area of the picture more than the colored areas of the outer and wider mat.

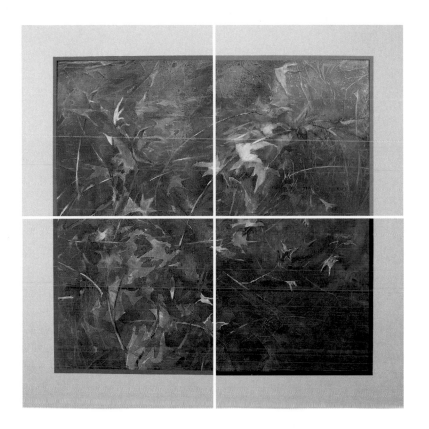

1	2
3	4

1. Strong effects can be created with a lighter outer mat and a darker inner mat. Blue "picks out" the blues in the background of the picture.

2. A less prominent choice—a green inner mat gives a more neutral darker-shaded effect than the blue.

3. A red inner mat is distracting. The viewer's eye is drawn to the thin stripe of color rather than the picture.

4. A black inner mat neatly outlines the picture.

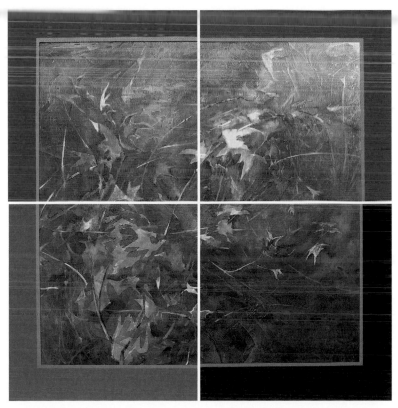

5	6
7	8

5. Bolder choices of color for outer mats, combined with a lighter inner mat, create markedly different effects to light outer mats and dark inner mats. Red is a dominant choice, overshadowing the more delicate tones present in the painting.

6. Blue is sympathetic to the overall tone of the painting and nicely echoes the colors of the background paint.

7. Green reflects some of the green tones in the image but feels a little "solid" next to the translucency of the paint.

8. Black is a little too "solid" and overpowering.

FRAMING A COLOR PICTURE

Now, by adding the option of using just a few frame types, the choices and subsequent effects for framing your image become almost infinite. Starting with a single choice of mat color, four frame styles are discussed.

1	2
3	4

1. A lilac-toned frame is used here due to areas of lilac color in the picture. The molding is only 1 inch (25mm) wide to prevent the frame dominating the picture. Also, this choice may not easily fit in with a neutral décor.

2. By using a 1¼–inch (30mm) gold profile with the cream mat, the autumnal effect of the image is enhanced.

3. A plain wooden frame, in this case a 2–inch (50mm) oak profile, tones down the golden colors.

4. A blue frame, 1¼ inches (30mm) wide, provides a contrast to the warm mat color.

1	2
3	4

1. The lilac frame and blue mat work quite harmoniously together but it is an uninspiring combination.

2. With the combination of the gold frame and the blue mat, the gold in the picture is picked out by the frame while the mat recedes.

3. The plain wood frame supplies a contrast to the blue mat. It's a calming combination that does not overpower the painting but complements it.

4. The blue mat looks good and suits the picture. However, it could be too cold with the blue frame.

1	2
3	4

1. The lilac frame and red mat do not clash too violently; however, the red is simply too intense and fights with the painting.

2. The use of red dominates the picture. The gold frame works reasonably well as it as strong as the red mat but is perhaps not the best combination overall.

3. Even with the neutral wood frame, red is too overpowering.

4. The blue frame and red mat fight for attention, not doing the painting any favors.

1	2
3	4

1. There is a fairly pleasing contrast between the green outer mat, cream inner mat, and the picture, but the lilac frame does nothing to enhance this combination.

2. The gold frame and green outer mat are a good combination but maybe the gold frame is just too showy for this picture?

3. The plain wood frame combined with a dark green outer mat and cream inner mat works nicely. It's a restful combination.

4. The blue frame and green outer mat are too similar in tone and give a muddy effect. The cream inner mat lifts it a little, but not enough.

Safety considerations

Goggles

Retractable knife blade

It is important to take into account safety considerations when picture framing, particularly when handling glass and using knives and other cutting tools.

As with most practical occupations, picture framing can be dangerous, and it's essential to take a few sensible precautions to prevent accidents.

Using knives and cutting tools

Your last thought before cutting anything should be "are my fingers in the way?" If the last thought through your mind is anything else, mistakes can occur that cause accidents, so before using a knife, mat cutter, or miter saw it's important to take stock of what you're doing.

When working with the various knives used in this book always use the safety covers supplied. Knives with retractable blades are recommended.

Scalpel with blade cover

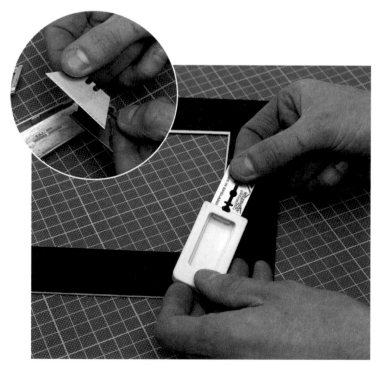

HANDLING LOOSE BLADES
When changing or handling loose blades, always handle them by the blunt and *not* the sharp edges.

USING KNIVES
When cutting with knives always keep them at as low an angle as possible to the board. Securing cutting edges in place with adhesive putty will reduce any chance of slipping while cutting.

Disposable
protective gloves

Heavy-duty safety gloves

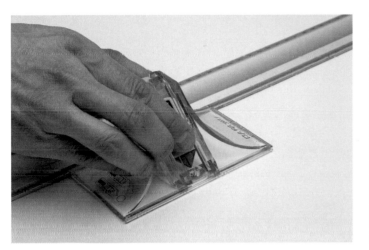

USING A MAT CUTTER
Always make sure the blades are retracted back into the body of
the mat cutters to prevent cutting yourself.

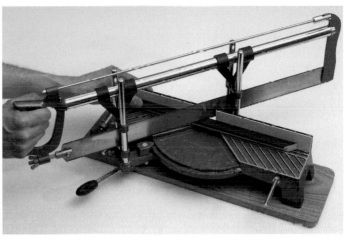

USING A MITER SAW
When using the miter saw or miter box to cut the molding, make
sure you keep your hand away from the blade. Use your other
hand to balance your body while holding the molding as this will
ease cutting and make the action safer.

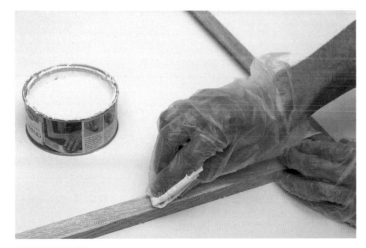

USING WAXES
When using waxes to finish off frames, be sure to use disposable,
protective gloves.

HANDLING GLASS
When handling glass, *always* wear suitable safety goggles to
prevent glass splinters entering your eyes and *always* wear
protective safety gloves to protect your hands.

chapter 2

Essential framing techniques

This chapter covers the fundamental techniques of picture framing. These techniques include how to cut an overmat, how to cut and miter a frame, cutting sheet glass, and fitting pictures into picture frames. Some of the more complicated tools will also be explained.

See also
Essential tools: *page 14*
Mats: *page 26*

Mat cutting

An overmat is a piece of colored board about $\frac{1}{16}$ inch (2mm) thick. It is used as a border for pictures and is designed to complement the image. The overmat has a 45-degree bevel that helps to lead the viewer's eye into the picture.

Hand-cut bevel

Begin cutting mats with an easy, smaller picture, a 6 x 4–inch (150 x 100mm) photo is a good size to start with. Purpose-made overmat cutters are also recommended as they provide a more even and accurate 45-degree bevel when compared to a mat cut with a knife and ruler.

Bevel cut with mat cutter

Tools and Materials

- **CHOSEN PHOTO**
- **STEEL RULER: 24 INCH (60CM)**
- **PENCIL WITH #2 LEAD OR HARDER**
- **SCRAP PAPER**
- **MATBOARD: 12 x 10 INCH (300 x 254MM)**
- **ADHESIVE PUTTY**
- **SELF-HEALING CUTTING MAT**
- **UTILITY KNIFE OR CRAFT KNIFE**
- **SANDPAPER**
- **MAT CUTTER**
- **RAZOR OR SCALPEL BLADE**
- **EMERY BOARD**
- **ERASER**

1 Measure the picture to be matted and make a note of this size. This is the "actual size." Now subtract $\frac{1}{8}$ inch (4mm) from this size to ascertain the "inside size." The inside size is always smaller than the "actual size" so that the picture does not drop through the overmat.

Sketch the mat

Make a diagram using these figures. Now add the 2½-inch (62mm) borders to the inside size to establish the "outside size" (this will also be the size that you will cut your glass, frame, and backing to).

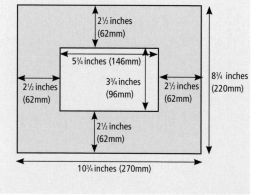

2½ inches (62mm)

5¾ inches (146mm)

3¾ inches (96mm)

2½ inches (62mm)

2½ inches (62mm)

8¾ inches (220mm)

2½ inches (62mm)

10¾ inches (270mm)

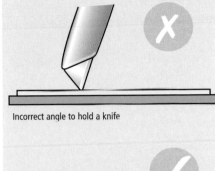

2 Mark your overmat board to the outside size using the pencil and steel ruler. Always work on back of the matboard, on what is usually the white side. Make sure that you know which is the colored side when using near-to-white colors.

3 Place the matboard on the cutting mat and cut along the steel ruler to create the 8¾ inch (220mm) width. After cutting the width, repeat for the 10¾ inch (270mm) length. You should now have one piece of matboard measuring 10¾ x 8¾ inches (270 x 220mm).

Knife safety

Always use the knife at as low an angle as possible so that it is fully under control. Your middle finger should drag along the matboard acting as a brake.

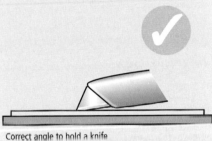

Incorrect angle to hold a knife

Correct angle to hold a knife

Measuring

Tip

Always make a rough sketch of the mat you are cutting because it helps to clarify what you are trying to achieve and eliminate mathematical mistakes. These are by far the most common mistakes that you are likely to make when cutting a mat.

When measuring, always make sure the steel ruler is positioned inside the markings you have just made. If you use two small pieces of adhesive putty on the underside of the ruler and then push the ruler down in line with the pencil marks, this will prevent the ruler from slipping while cutting.

4 You can now mark out the aperture on the back of the card. To do this measure 2½ inches (62mm) in from the outside edge of the matboard on all four sides. Make two marks on each of the four sides, then join up the lines.

5 As a further check on size, place your image on the back of the matboard you have prepared. If the guidelines you have marked out are just covered, then you know your mat aperture will fit the picture.

Tip

Before you use your mat cutter, you will need to rub down the sharp plastic edges on its underside with sandpaper. This will prevent the mat cutter base from catching on the matboard.

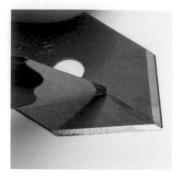

6 On the mat cutter blade, add a pencil line as above. This line is important because it indicates where to start and stop cutting with the mat cutter.

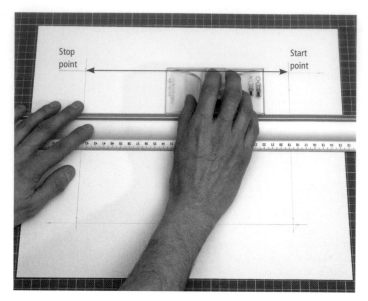

Using the mat cutter

Do not apply too much pressure as you move the mat cutter. Once you reach the stop point, keep the blade at the same depth and then slide the mat cutter back to the start point. Only then should you move the blade slightly deeper and then repeat the cutting stage. The blade should get visibly deeper but the pencil line should always be in line with the starting point for each successive cut.

The sequence for cutting each line of the overmat aperture is:
1. Position the mat cutter in the start position.
2. Slide the blade into the matboard.
3. Slide the mat cutter along to the stop position while applying even pressure on the blade.
4. Keep blade at same depth and return to the start position.
5. Slide the blade deeper into the matboard.
6. Repeat steps 3–5.

With practice, you will know how many cuts you need to make to cut right through the matboard. This will vary from person to person but do not cut through in less than six sweeps. When you think you are through the matboard, slide the mat cutter along to the start point and you may be able gently to lift the outer border of the mat. If there is a clear gap along the line you have just cut, you are through! If not, try one more sweep.

7 Now line up the mat cutter with the first line to be cut on the back of the matboard. Be careful to make sure the mat cutter is properly positioned, so that it does not cut above or below the line.

8 Slide the mat cutter along to the starting point. Now slide the blade down into the matboard in alignment with the pencil line, but only penetrate the first layer of card. When this is done, move the mat cutter along the line until the pencil line on the blade lines up with the stop point. This is the first of six to eight sweeps or cuts all made in the same direction. When cutting, keep a small amount of pressure on the sliding blade but only enough to keep it at a uniform depth all the way along the cut.

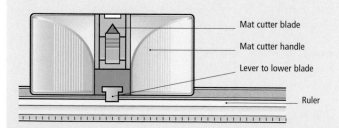

Mat cutter blade

Mat cutter handle

Lever to lower blade

Ruler

9 When you have successfully cut the first line of the aperture, you can repeat the process for the remaining three lines. It is recommended that you cut the two longest lines first, followed by the two shorter lines. It is at this point that you benefit from sanding down the base of the mat cutter. If it was not sanded, the mat cutter would catch on the burr created by the first two cuts.

10 Once all four sides are cut, very carefully turn over the matboard while supporting the middle with one hand, and the cut section should come away from the overmat easily. However, it is likely that there will be some fibers in the corners holding the middle of the matboard in the aperture. Don't just push the middle out as it will tear the matboard. Instead, taking great care, slide a razor or scalpel blade down into the gap between the aperture and border. Then slide it along until it frees the piece of matboard.

11 You may find that you have a burr along the top edge of the bevel on the colored side of the matboard. This can be smoothed down by carefully rubbing the side of your thumbnail along the top of the bevel. While doing this, keep your wrist/hand on the border of the mat to steady your hand so it does not slip across the face of the matboard. Smooth down any rough edges on the bevel with an emery board.

Now position the mat over the photo and see what it looks like.

See also
Attaching the picture to the mat:
page 44

Wet mounting

Frequently, the works that you wish to frame will not have been executed directly onto paper that's thick or firm enough to support them without backing material being added, so you will need to mount the works onto matboard. However, before you permanently mount something, you should first consider its impact on the value of the artwork.

Photographs can be mounted on matboard prior to framing.

Most of the pictures you frame will be printed, painted, or drawn on paper. This could be photographic paper, print paper, posters, certificates, and original works of art. Paper can sometimes buckle in the picture frame when it is exposed to extremes of temperature change (from summer to winter or when the heating is turned on and off) or moisture in the atmosphere. If the artwork to be framed is attached properly to the overmat, as described in "Attaching the picture to the mat," page 44, this should not happen. However, your artwork may already be wrinkled, creased, or rolled tightly and you may want to attach the artwork to a board to prevent further creasing.

Tools and Materials

- **SPRAY ADHESIVE**
- **MATBOARD**
- **OLD NEWSPAPER OR CARDSTOCK**
- **COTTON CLOTH**
- **RULER**
- **ADHESIVE PUTTY**
- **KNIFE**

1 Cut a piece of matboard at least 4 inches (100mm) bigger than the outside measurement of the picture. Use adhesive putty to secure the ruler while cutting the card.

2 Using old newspaper or a piece of cardstock, cover the workbench area to avoid spraying the surface with adhesive. Next, place the picture to be wet mounted upside down on the newspaper and spray the back of the paper. Make sure to shake the can thoroughly before spraying and test the flow of the aerosol on a scrap of cardstock before spraying the back of the picture.

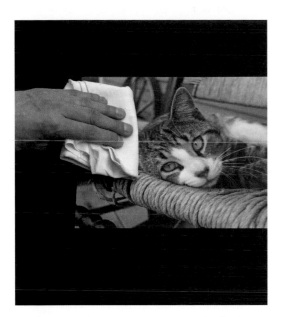

3 Once there is an even coating of adhesive on the picture, place the picture onto the matboard. Using the cotton cloth, gently apply pressure to the picture with a swabbing action, *not* a sweeping action. Take care not transfer any excess of spray adhesive from the cloth onto the picture when working the cloth near the edge of the paper.

4 Leave the picture to dry on the board in preparation for attaching the overmat, if you are using one. If not, trim down the edges of the board to the outside size of the frame, ready to be fitted into it.

To mount or not to mount?

Your picture may look more presentable if wet mounted onto a thicker board, because this process will prevent it from buckling in the frame and becoming unsightly. However, if your picture has any financial value it is not recommended that it is wet mounted. If the artwork is attached to a board, it is no longer "in its original state"; the process of wet mounting will have effectively devalued your picture. All this means that the process of wet mounting should only be considered if the picture is of no financial value. An alternative method of removing creases is to ask a professional picture framer to press your picture. This may reduce some creasing but will not necessarily eliminate it.

The picture could be dry mounted using reversible materials. This is a process that uses heat-activated tissues that can be re-heated to reverse the process. A heat- or-pressure activated tissue is used instead of a spray adhesive (the principle is the same as a hem seal for adjusting the length of pants). The picture is placed on top of a piece of tissue, which is then placed on top of a thicker board. This "package" is then pressed using a large heated press for heat-activated tissue, or rollers for pressure-activated tissues. The process results in very flat pictures, but anything of financial worth has been radically altered from its original state so do keep this in mind when considering dry mounting your pictures.

Dry mounting press

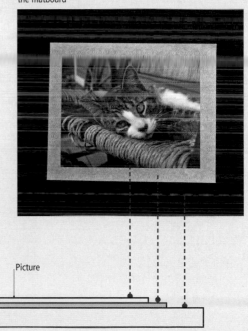

The tissue is placed between the picture and the matboard

Matboard   Heat-activated tissue   Picture

See also
Wet mounting: *page 42*

Attaching the picture to the mat

The picture needs to be attached to the mat so that it is secure and does not become loose in the frame. The method used must also keep the picture from becoming wrinkled when in the frame, and prevent any permanent damage to the artwork.

There are two techniques demonstrated here. The first is for pictures on paper and the alternative method is for pictures already on a board that is at least as thick as a piece of matboard, being about ⅟₁₆ inch (1.5mm) thick. The alternative method should not be used on thin paper pictures because the gummed paper tape will cause the paper to buckle around the edges and will make your pictures crease, or even tear in time. If you want to first mount your picture on matboard, see "Wet mounting," page 42.

Tip

Use only gummed paper tape to attach your pictures. Don't use self-adhesive tapes such as masking tape, parcel tape, clear sticky tape, or insulating tape. These will quickly dry out and peel away. The glues used in these tapes can also leave acidic residue that can show through to the front of the picture.

Tools and Materials

- GUMMED PAPER TAPE
- SCISSORS OR UTILITY KNIFE
- RULER
- SMALL PIECE OF SPONGE
- BOWL OF WATER

For pictures on thin paper

1 Position the picture upside down on the workbench so that 1 inch (25mm) of the top of the picture overhangs the edge of the bench. Then position your overmat over the picture. When positioning a picture, be sure to take into consideration the artist's signature. Also, measure the white borders on the picture with a ruler to ensure you have even amounts of white showing.

2 Cut off two pieces of gummed paper tape about 1½–2 inches (38–50mm) long. Wet them one at a time with the sponge and water. Then, keeping the picture in the correct position on the mat with the palm of one hand, look underneath the picture and place one piece of gummed paper tape on the top of the print at each end.

3 Turn the mat and the picture over and burnish the tape down to ensure a strong grip on the paper. This effectively "hinges" the picture to the mat. The picture will expand and contract in heat, but the position of the two pieces of tape allows for this and the picture will not wrinkle.

The picture should now be securely attached to the mat.

Alternative method

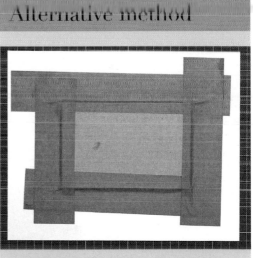

Follow steps 1–3, opposite for pictures on thin paper. At the end of step 3, cut off four pieces of gummed paper tape about 2 inches (50mm) longer than the length and width of the picture. Secure these extra pieces of gummed paper tape as above.

See also
Essential tools: *page 14*

Setting up the miter saw

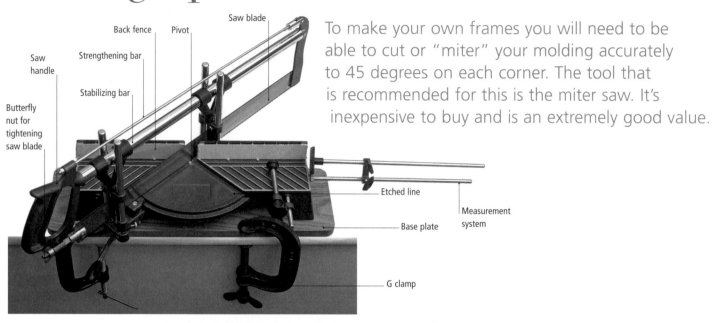

Saw blade

Back fence · Pivot

Saw handle · Strengthening bar

Stabilizing bar

Butterfly nut for tightening saw blade

Etched line

Measurement system

Base plate

G clamp

To make your own frames you will need to be able to cut or "miter" your molding accurately to 45 degrees on each corner. The tool that is recommended for this is the miter saw. It's inexpensive to buy and is an extremely good value.

Tools and Materials

- **MITER SAW**
- **ADHESIVE PUTTY**
- **TWO SMALL STRIPS OF MATBOARD**
- **STEEL RULER: 24 INCH (60CM)**
- **PENCIL WITH #2 LEAD OR HARDER**
- **BRADAWL**
- **FOUR G CLAMPS**

1 Attach the saw blade guide onto the miter saw base. Ensure that the pivot on which the saw rotates is tightened so that the saw is not loose in its bracket.

2 Assemble the miter saw so that the saw is secured to the base plate.

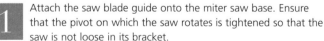

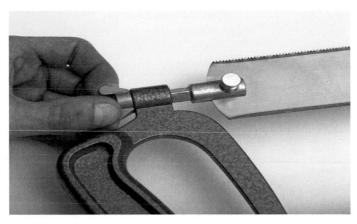

3 Attach the blade to the miter saw handle. Ensure that the blade is attached to the saw the right way round so that the teeth of the blade point away from the handle. Ensure the saw moves freely along its bracket. Most saw blades are designed so that the teeth point away from the handle. This is so that the saw actually cuts when the blade is pushed away from the body. Then when the blade is pulled back, any resulting dust is cleared from the cut to allow for the next cut.

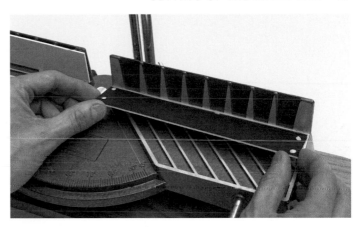

4 Using adhesive putty, secure two narrow strips of matboard to the back fence of the miter saw to prevent the aluminum ribs from denting the soft wood moldings.

5 Add an etched line onto the base of the miter saw. Position the ruler so that it lines up with the center of the pivot on which the saw rotates and the 45-degree marker on the angle scale of the saw. Secure the ruler with adhesive putty so that it does not move. Score along the ruler with the bradawl to make a clearly visible line. When these lines are added, it will become clear exactly where the saw blade will cut. These lines will be used to line up the picture frame molding when measuring the lengths.

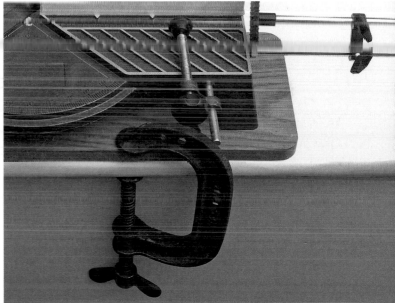

6 Secure the miter saw to the workbench with either one G clamp in the middle or one at each end of the base plate. The miter saw is now ready for cutting the picture frame molding.

See also
Essential tools: *page 14*
Setting up the miter saw: *page 46*

Frame cutting using a miter saw

Now that the miter saw is correctly assembled it can be used to cut the picture frame molding. A worked example of a 12 x 10–inch (305 x 254mm) frame will be used for this section.

Tip

When buying your molding you will need to add 3 inches (75mm) to each dimension of the frame size. This extra length allows enough molding to turn the saw around and cut the other end.

Tools and Materials

- **MITER SAW**
- **STEEL RULER: 24 INCH (60CM)**
- **PENCIL WITH #2 LEAD OR HARDER**
- **SUITABLE MOLDING FOR YOUR PICTURE**
- **EMERY BOARD OR SMALL PIECE OF FINE SANDPAPER**

The miter saw will be used to make a total of eight cuts—four in one direction at 45 degrees and four in the other direction at 45 degrees. Make sure that the miter saw is always "clicked" into place on the 45-degree marker on the angle scale to ensure accuracy.

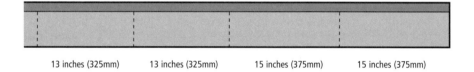

13 inches (325mm)   13 inches (325mm)   15 inches (375mm)   15 inches (375mm)

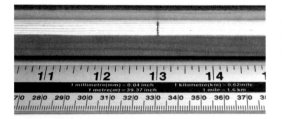

1 Remembering to add 3 inches (75mm) to each length, mark out the four sides of your frame along the length of molding. The molding will need to be marked out along the inside depth of the rabbet with four clear vertical lines to align the miter saw to for each side of the frame.

Picture frame molding

The rabbet is the part of the molding that prevents the glass, overmat (if used), picture, and backing from falling straight through the front of the frame. On the right is a length of molding that has been cut, or mitered, at 45 degrees. The rabbet of the molding is marked with a dotted line. This is the part of the molding you always measure along with your ruler.

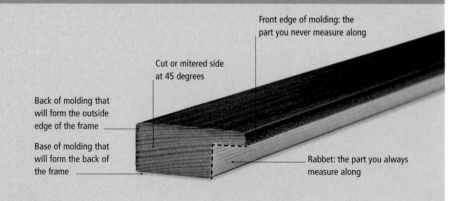

Front edge of molding: the part you never measure along

Cut or mitered side at 45 degrees

Back of molding that will form the outside edge of the frame

Base of molding that will form the back of the frame

Rabbet: the part you always measure along

2 Place the molding on the miter saw base with the back of the molding up against the back fence of the miter saw. Position the molding so that the first line you have marked out on the molding lines up directly with the lines you have etched on the miter saw base.

3 Clamp the molding in place to the miter saw base. Use a G clamp to secure the molding if your saw only has one clamp. To avoid crushing the rabbet of the frame with the clamp, place a pencil underneath the rabbet for support.

Clamping the molding into the saw

Do not tighten the G clamps or the clamps on the miter saw straight onto the rabbet of the frame as this will dent it. The clamp needs to grip onto the bottom of the rabbet, so, by placing a pencil under it, the clamps will grip the molding without damaging it.

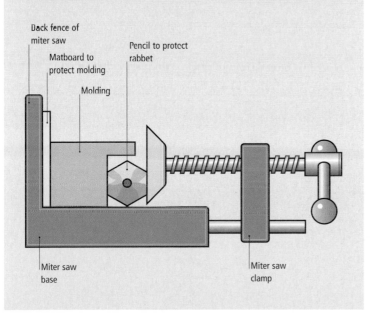

Back fence of miter saw

Matboard to protect molding

Pencil to protect rabbet

Molding

Miter saw base

Miter saw clamp

4 Gently lower the saw onto the molding ready to cut. Pull the saw backward for the first few strokes to ensure a neat start to the cut. Use only slow, gentle movements to avoid inaccurate cuts.

5 Repeat the cutting technique in step 4 for the other three cuts. You should now have four pieces of molding—this is the halfway stage. Now, turn the saw around again making sure it "clicks" into the 45-degree notch on its base.

45-degree miter | Molding on its side | Mark a vertical line on the rabbet at 12¹⁄₁₆ inches (302mm)

Measure from the edge of the miter | Ruler | Rabbet

6 Mark out the first piece of molding to the length required. Cut out the longest dimension of the frame first. For the example used, cut the 12 inch (300mm) length first because if a mistake is made on the long measurement this length can always be used for a short side instead. Remember the dimension has to have ¹⁄₁₆ inch (2mm) added to it to allow for expansion of materials or contraction of the frame. Also, the glass will need to be slightly smaller than the frame so as to avoid breaking the glass with too tight a fit. Therefore the molding needs to have a vertical line marked on the rabbet of the molding at 12¹⁄₁₆ inches (302mm).

7 Now, when you have aligned the pencil line on the molding with the etched line on the miter saw clamp the molding into the saw.

8 Cut the molding to length using the same cutting technique as in step 4. Once you have cut through the molding leave the saw in position at the bottom of the cut.

9 Now attach the measuring system to the left-hand end of the saw base and slide it along until it meets the end of your piece of molding. Tighten the screw on the measuring system and remove your first piece of molding. Then take off the saw and butt your second long side of molding up to the measuring system. Clamp it in place and cut the second long side.

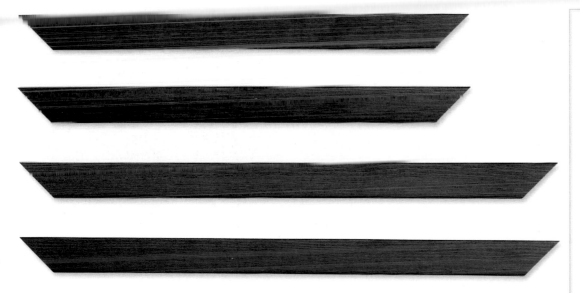

10 Repeat steps 6–9 for the short sides of your frame. You should now have four pieces of molding ready to assemble.

Tip

You will create a lot of sawdust and it will probably hinder the view of the etched line on the miter saw base. Do not blow this dust as it will invariably go in your eyes. The best idea is to keep the sawdust in a small pot or box and use it as a filler in combination with wood glue (see "Frame assembly" on page 52).

See also
Essential tools: *page 14*
Moldings: *page 20*

Frame assembly

Miter vises

This section shows you how to assemble a frame using a miter vise and wood glue in combination with nails.

Miter vises vary in size and strength and you need to make sure you buy one that will fit your chosen molding. Most will take a molding at least 2 inches (50mm) wide. Also be aware that the metal vises will easily dent the back of your wooden molding, so use two scrap pieces of matboard between the jaws of the vise and your molding to prevent this damage.

Tools and Materials

- ROUGH SURFACE TAPE
- MITER VISE (TWO IF POSSIBLE)
- GENERAL PURPOSE LUBRICATING OIL
- G CLAMP
- SCREWDRIVER AND SCREWS (OPTIONAL— IF YOU'RE GOING TO ATTACH THE MITER VISE TO YOUR WORKBENCH)
- HAND DRILL
- 1–INCH (25MM) NAILS (19-GAUGE OR PANEL PINS)
- YOUR MITERED MOLDING
- TWO SCRAP PIECES OF MATBOARD
- WOOD GLUE
- PAPER TOWEL
- TACK HAMMER
- EMERY BOARD/CLOTH
- COLORED FELT-TIPPED PEN OR PASTEL CRAYON

1 Attach small pieces of rough surface tape to the jaws of the vise. The rough surface tape will grip the molding during assembly, preventing it from slipping. It is also worth putting a drop of oil onto the threads of the vise and making sure it works easily. One complete opening and closing of the vise will lubricate it. You are now ready to assemble your frame.

2 Secure one miter vise to the workbench. The vise can be G clamped to the bench or screwed to it if it does not matter if your workbench has two permanent screw holes in it. (If you are using two miter vises you only need to secure one as the second will always be in a different position for different size frames.)

Tip

You can also join your frames with an underpinner but these machines are expensive. The cheaper underpinners tend to join the corners perfectly at the base of the miter but create an unsightly gap at the top.

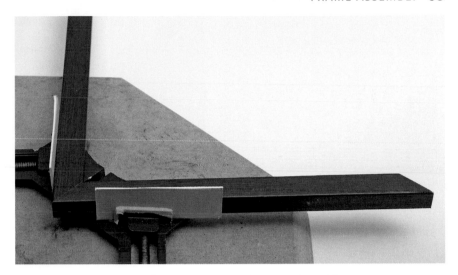

4 Using one long length and one short length, clamp the moldings into the vise to form a corner of the frame. Try to get into the habit of putting the "long side on left, short side on right" to avoid an easy mistake. Place the scrap pieces of matboard between the vise jaws and the molding. This will prevent any denting of the molding. Make sure the moldings are sitting in the vise properly before tightening.

3 Prepare the hand drill. Use a nail in the chuck as a drill "bit." This means you do not need an expensive drill bit that might not be the right size. Also if your nail bends or breaks you have plenty more to hand.

Positioning the molding in the vise

You must ensure that the molding is positioned correctly in the vise, or you might damage the molding.

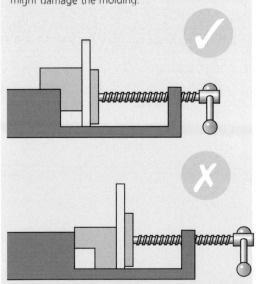

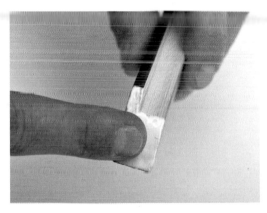

5 When you are satisfied that the corner lines up correctly, take out the long side leaving the short side in the vise. By leaving one side in the vise in the correct position it will be easier to realign when glue is applied to the other length. Now apply some wood glue onto the molding you have removed from the vise.

Tip

It is recommended that you use only water-based wood glue, such as craft glue or white wood glue. Do not use instant contact glues or strong industrial spirit-based glues. This is because it is quite difficult to align two pieces of molding perfectly in the miter vise and you may need to make slight adjustments to ensure a perfectly aligned corner. Also, the glue often spills over onto the top of the frame. (In fact, this seepage is good because it ensures there's plenty of glue.) A spirit glue might take the surface off your molding.

Gluing the miter

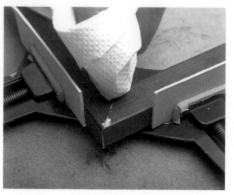

Use plenty of glue because most wooden moldings are very porous and the glue will quickly sink into the wood leaving hardly any on the surface to create the bond. There should be an excess of glue and it should spill over onto the top of the molding to ensure enough glue for a secure bond.

Use your finger to ensure every area of the surface has some glue on it. You can see now why you should not use strong contact adhesives—you would simply glue your finger to the molding!

6 Place the molding you removed back in the vise and align with the other side. Wipe off any excess glue.

Tip

The action of the nails converging actually forces the corner together to form a tighter miter. Also, it is harder for the corner to be forced apart with the nails converging on each other.

7 Using the hand drill with the nail as a drill bit, drill two holes in the side of the frame. Try to make the holes converge so that it forces the miter together.

8 Once the holes are drilled, insert the nails and tap them in slowly with the hammer. Leave the corner in the vise while the glue dries. This is where having two miter vises is helpful. If you can work with the other two molding pieces in a second vise the time you will have to wait for the glue to dry will be shortened.

9 Now repeat steps 3–8 for the remaining two pieces. Be sure to have the long side on the same side as the other pair. Again, think "long side on left, short side on right" to avoid an easy mistake of frame assembly.

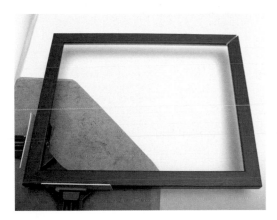

Disguising the nails

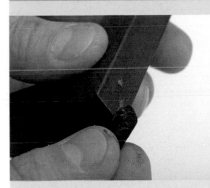

10 If you have two vises, nail the final two corners at the same time to save on drying time for the glue, if not, you'll have to nail them individually. Make sure you apply glue to both of the remaining miters.

11 Once the frame is assembled, use an emery board or emery cloth to gently sand down any rough edges on the outside of the frame. If you have any gaps at the back of your miters, push a little glue into the gap before sanding.

Although the visibility of the nails can be an issue for some people, you should not try to sink the nails right into the molding. This is because this drastically reduces the amount of nail holding the corner together until the glue dries. Also, you would need to fill the nail holes, which would require more equipment, such as wood fillers, and then trying to match the molding may make more of an unsightly corner than the barely visible nails. You can always color the nail heads with felt-tipped pens.

It's useful to have a selection of felt-tipped pens for different frames. For gold/silver frames you can use gold and silver pens but be careful that the spirit-based ink does not remove the color on the frame. Shoe polish or woodstain can be used for stained wood frames. Try the pen on a piece of scrap first to see the effect on your chosen molding.

For the finished piece, lightly color in the bare wood resulting from the filing with a suitable colored felt-tipped pen or pastel crayon.

See also
Safety considerations: *page 34*

Glass cutting

It is highly recommended that you take your finished picture frames to your local glaziers and get them to cut the glass for you. This has the advantage of increased safety as you are not handling the glass and less waste as you won't be cutting down large sheets of glass yourself. However, it is useful to know how to cut and trim glass. If you make a mistake and find that the glass does not quite fit the frame you can cut it down and use it for another frame.

Tip

Glass can be very dangerous to work with. Sheets of glass are quite large and are difficult to handle. You should always wear safety goggles to protect your eyes and safety gloves to protect your hands.

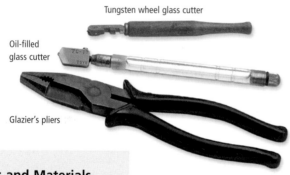

Tungsten wheel glass cutter

Oil-filled
glass cutter

Glazier's pliers

There are three main types of glass cutter, diamond-headed (used for heavy-duty glass), tungsten, and steel wheel-headed cutters, the latter being the most readily available. They normally have six or more wheels mounted on a wooden shaft. When a wheel becomes blunt it can be rotated so that a new one takes its place. Even so, they do not last very long. Tungsten wheels, which are not much more expensive, last far longer. For most frames, $\frac{1}{16}$–inch (2mm) glass, which is light and reasonably strong, is used. For very large areas of glass in a frame you may have to purchase either heavy-duty, $\frac{1}{4}$–inch (6mm) glass or perspex. Beyond about 40 inches (1m) square, light $\frac{1}{16}$–inch (2mm) glass is difficult to hold and can wobble in the middle and break. Thicker glass is recommended for frames of this size.

Tools and Materials

- **SAFETY GOGGLES**
- **SAFETY GLOVES**
- **GLASS (REQUIRED AMOUNT AND THICKNESS FOR YOUR FRAME)**
- **WOOD RULER**
- **FELT-TIPPED PEN**
- **T-SQUARE (IF CUTTING LARGE SHEETS OF GLASS)**
- **ADHESIVE PUTTY**
- **GLASS CUTTER**
- **GENERAL PURPOSE LUBRICATING OIL (FOR OIL-FILLED GLASS CUTTER)**
- **MINERAL SPIRIT (FOR TUNGSTEN WHEEL CUTTER)**
- **GLASS-CUTTING PLIERS**

Cutting glass for rectangular frames

1 Glass can be measured in the normal way with a ruler and T-square, but in this case the frame has already been joined, so the glass is held against the back of the frame and marked with a felt-tipped pen.

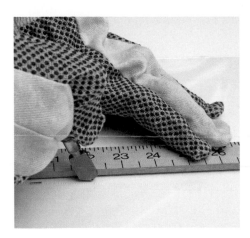

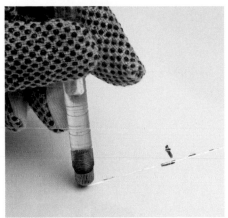

2 Make sure the cutting surface is smooth, as any lumps or bumps underneath will shatter the glass as you cut. Place a wood ruler on the line. Lubricate the glass-cutting wheel in oil, white spirit, or methylated spirit, and score the glass. Practice on some scrap glass first so that you can find out how much pressure to apply. Only make one cut or score, and do not go back over the same line as this will quickly blunt the glass-cutting wheel. It will also make the cut uneven and create very sharp glass splinters.

3 Most pictures under glass are framed with the standard 1/16–inch (2mm) glass, which does not require a lot of pressure. After scoring the glass, tap vigorously along the line of the cut. This makes it easier to break the glass cleanly. Many cutters have a round knob at the end of the stem for tapping the glass.

4 With care, turn the piece of glass over and break the glass along the scored line. Here the glass is held with the thumbs on either side of the scored line and pressure is exerted from both sides. This should break the glass easily.

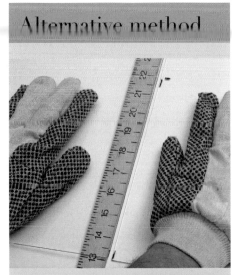

Alternative method

5 Sometimes the glass needs to be trimmed. Small pieces can't be broken in the same way because there is insufficient surface area, so special glass-breaking pliers are used, placed on the score line. If the glass doesn't break in one long piece, persevere along the cut, breaking off small sections at a time.

Another method of breaking glass, that is safer than holding it in your hands, is to place it on a flat ruler or straight edge and press either side. The scored mark must be very closely aligned to the edge of the ruler before downward pressure is exerted.

Cutting glass for oval frames

Glass for oval frames is cut in the same way as it is for rectangular frames, by scoring and snapping. There are professional oval and circle glass cutters, but these are too expensive for occasional use. The score should be made in one continuous motion; however, in all probability you will not be able to release the oval's surround in one piece. It's advisable to make some additional tangential cuts to the edge of the glass so that it can be broken away in small pieces.

1 Here, an oval frame is being used as a template. Place the piece of glass over the back of the oval frame and, using a felt-tipped pen, mark a start point on the glass where it crosses the rabbet of the oval frame.

2 Score around the frame just inside the rabbet to allow the glass to fit. It is best to do this scoring in one continuous motion, so position the glass and oval frame on the corner of your bench and effectively "walk around" the frame. (Make sure they are secure on the bench.) Practice the sweeping motion before you cut to be sure of an unobstructed path.

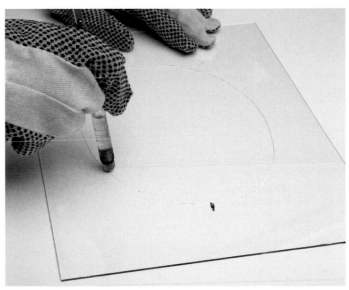

3 When you arrive back at the start point made with the felt-tipped pen, continue cutting to the edge of the glass to form a tangent to the curve.

4 Once the glass has been scored all the way round, take the frame out from underneath the glass and tap vigorously on the score line with the other end of your glass cutter to loosen the oval shape from the surrounding glass. The glass should appear to crack along the scored line as you tap.

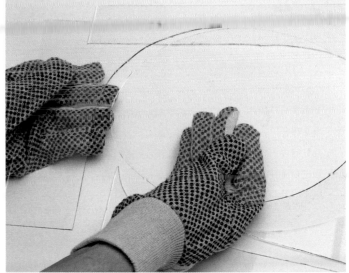

5 If scoring and tapping does not release the oval, make a series of cuts from the edge of the oval to the outside edge of the glass. These sections can then be broken off piece-by-piece around the oval.

6 Apply slight pressure with your hands to break away the separate pieces of glass to release the oval in the center.

See also
Mat cutting: *page 38*
Glass cutting: *page 56*

Tools and Materials

- **BACKING BOARD CUT TO SIZE**
- **BACKING SHEET CUT TO SIZE**
- **STEEL RULER**
- **UTILITY KNIFE OR CRAFT KNIFE WITH NEW SHARP BLADE**
- **GLASS CUTTING TOOLS (IF CUTTING GLASS YOURSELF, SEE PAGE 56)**
- **GLASS CUT TO SIZE**
- **BLANKET OR THICK CLOTH (TO PLACE ON THE WORKBENCH TO PROTECT THE FRAME)**
- **CHAMOIS**
- **COTTON CLOTH**
- **GLASS CLEANER**
- **FINE-GRADE STEEL WOOL**
- **OVERMAT**
- **CLEAR ADHESIVE TAPE OR CONSERVATION/ ARCHIVAL/ACID-FREE TAPE**
- **SCRAP PIECE OF MATBOARD**
- **19-GAUGE PANEL PINS OR NAILS**
- **TACK HAMMER**
- **SCRAP PIECE OF WOOD**
- **G CLAMP**
- **GUMMED PAPER TAPE**
- **SCISSORS**
- **SMALL PIECE OF SPONGE**
- **BOWL OF WATER**
- **BRADAWL**

Fitting picture frames

Fitting pictures into your picture frames can be time consuming, mainly due to small pieces of dust that become trapped and visible behind the picture glass. Therefore, before fitting, make sure you thoroughly clean your workbench to keep unwanted dust to a minimum.

Tip

Why use backing sheet? Backing sheet is designed to create a layer of less acidic, or "neutral pH," material between the picture and the backing board. This helps to protect the picture from impurities that may be in the lesser quality backing boards that are used.

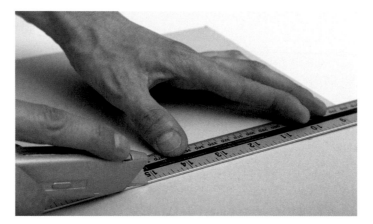

1 Cut pieces of backing board and backing sheet to size (they should be the same size as the matboard, or the "outside" size). The best backing board to use is 1/16–inch (2mm) grayboard or millboard as it is probably the easiest to cut, gives a smooth finish, and makes the least amount of dust. Other alternatives are medium-density fiberboard (MDF), hardboard, plyboard, or simply use matboard. Make sure you secure the ruler to the boards with adhesive putty to prevent the ruler from slipping.

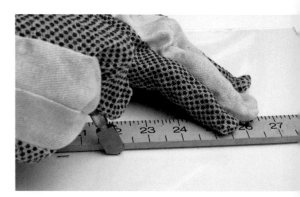

2 Commission a glazier to cut some glass or cut a piece of glass to fit your picture yourself (see "Glass cutting," pages 56–59).

3 Now, clean both sides of the glass. If your workbench has a slippery surface cover it with a thick (non-hairy) cloth to place the glass on; this will also help to keep your workbench dust-free. The best way to clean glass is to use a damp chamois and then a dry cotton cloth. It is best to clean the glass very slowly so that you do not catch the edge with your cloth and cause it to slide suddenly across your workbench. Slow wiping movements are recommended. If you are using old glass from an old frame, you can use a piece of very fine-grade steel wool for the more persistent marks.

4 Place the picture attached to the overmat on top of the backing and backing sheet. Then place the glass on top of the picture. This is referred to as the picture framing "sandwich." Check for obvious pieces of dust or dirt in between the picture and the glass. If there is any, simply hinge or lift the piece of glass up as you would a lid on a hinged box. This is the safest way to handle the glass at this stage. Remove the offending piece of dust or dirt and try again.

The picture framing "sandwich"

The "sandwich" sounds like an odd idea but it really does help to keep the dust out. It will also help to keep out thunderbugs. These are tiny bugs that seem to take to the air whenever there is a storm brewing. Basically they get everywhere in your house (especially if you live in the countryside) and often crawl in between the glass and the picture in picture frames. Have a look at slightly older picture frames and see if there are any tiny marks on the overmat or picture. If there are, they are probably thunderbugs. By sealing the picture in, the bugs get stuck to the tape and can't cause any problems.

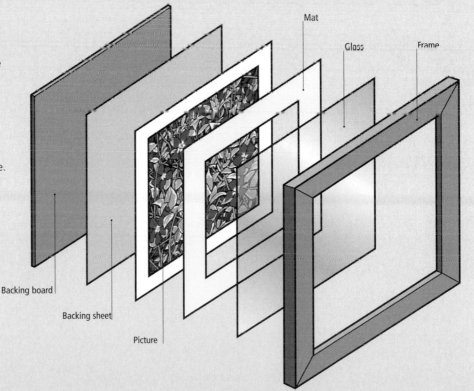

Backing board

Backing sheet

Picture

Mat

Glass

Frame

5 Seal around the sandwich with clear adhesive tape or a suitable conservation/archival/acid-free tape. Cut off a length of tape that is slightly longer than the side of glass you are using. Overlap the edge of the glass with the tape by about 1/16 inch (2mm) so that it will not be visible from the front of the picture frame. This amount of overlap should be hidden under the rabbet of the frame. Then wrap it around so that it forms a seal around the sandwich.

Tip

It can be frustrating to fit your picture and then discover stray pieces of dirt when the picture frame is hung on the wall. Therefore make sure your fitting area is well lit. A portable spot light may help to illuminate the workbench to make all unwanted dust or dirt easily visible.

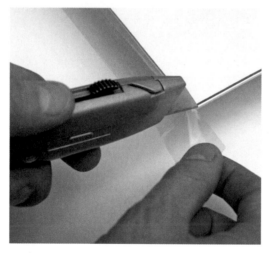

6 Now turn the sandwich around and check for any dust. If there is any, just lift up the glass as in step 4 (the tape is now effectively a hinge) and remove the offending piece of dust. Once you are happy that it is dust-free, place the frame over the sandwich to ensure that it still fits the frame and that every part of the sandwich is properly aligned. If it does not now fit the frame, you will need to remove one of the pieces of tape and realign the sandwich.

7 Once you have sealed two opposing sides of the sandwich, you may have more pieces of dust trapped under the glass. To remove this dust without removing the pieces of tape, cut off a thin slice of matboard, about 1/2 inch (12mm) wide by about 12 inches (305mm) long. By gently easing the matboard or the picture away from the glass on the sides that you haven't taped yet, you may be able to reach the piece of dust with the matboard offcut and hook it out. Once achieved, seal the remaining two sides of the sandwich.

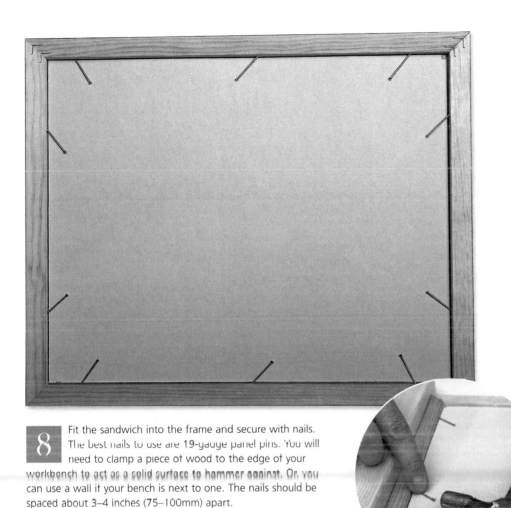

8 Fit the sandwich into the frame and secure with nails. The best nails to use are 19-gauge panel pins. You will need to clamp a piece of wood to the edge of your workbench to act as a solid surface to hammer against. Or, you can use a wall if your bench is next to one. The nails should be spaced about 3–4 inches (75–100mm) apart.

Using a point driving gun

You may want to use a point-driving gun especially made for this part of picture framing. They are reasonably expensive but if you are fitting quite a few frames it may be a worthwhile investment. If you use this tool, position a block of wood on the outside of the frame to act as leverage to reduce the shock on the frame from the point-driver's recoil.

Narrow pictures

If you are fitting larger pictures with narrow moldings, such as a long school photo or a long thin poster, you can prevent the frame from bowing by creating a hook with your nails in the middle of the long sides.

1 Hammer the nail so that it enters the backing board at a very low angle to the backing board. If the angle is too large you will go through the backing and it could possibly go through your picture and break your glass.

2 Once the nail is halfway in, hit it from the side to bend it around to form a hook. This will keep the backing tight against the long side and also prevent bowing in the future.

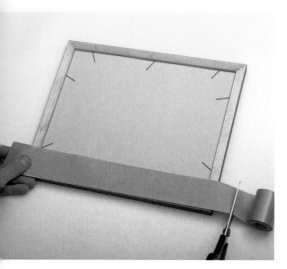

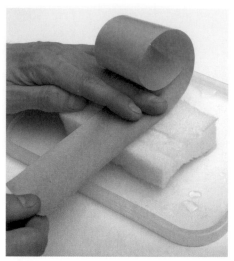

9 Using the scissors, cut a piece of gummed paper tape slightly longer than one side of the frame.

10 Dip the sponge into the bowl of water. Using one hand, place one end of the gummed paper tape on the sponge, while applying pressure to the top of the tape with your other hand and drag the length across the sponge. Make sure the tape is very wet as it will easily peel off if not enough water is used.

11 Quickly place the gummed paper tape along the edge of the frame. Make sure it is about ⅟₁₆ inch (2mm) in from the outer edge of the frame. Use a cloth to press the tape evenly.

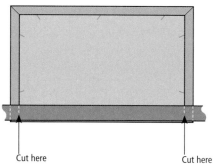

Cut here   Cut here

12 If there is a gap in height between the back of the frame and the backing board, make a cut down the inside edges of the gummed paper tape in the corners of the frame with a knife and then press the tape onto the backing again with a cloth. If the tape is not sticking it is better to tear it off and start again with another, wetter piece.

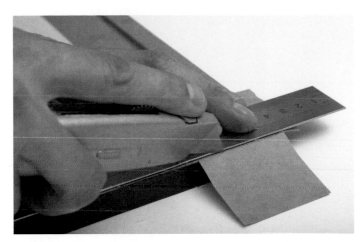

13 When you have taped in all four sides, use a ruler and a knife to trim off the excess gummed paper tape at the corners. Use a utility knife, making sure not to slip down the side of the frame with the knife.

The back of the finished frame should now look like this.

chapter 3

Hanging pictures

In this chapter the methods by which pictures can be hung—using the available fixtures and fittings—are explored. Also discussed are the aesthetic considerations of where and in what formation to hang pictures in an interior, as well how to light your pictures once they're on the wall.

Hanging pictures

To successfully hang pictures you will need to use a combination of hooks on the back of the frame with wire or picture cord tied between them. Then you will need to have a secure hook on the wall to hang it from.

The standard method for hanging pictures is to tie cord or wire between two hooks screwed into the frame. For small to medium sized pictures use small screw eyes or screw rings (a screw eye with a key ring attached). For medium to heavy pictures D rings or double D rings can be screwed to the frame. For really heavy pictures, glass plates can be screwed to the frame and then the frame screwed onto the wall through the glass plate. A final consideration is the type of wall your picture will hang on. The nails that are supplied with X hooks are very strong and should penetrate most solid walls. If you have cavity walls you will need to drill and fit the hole with a wall plug. Double X hooks can be used in this instance by screwing through the heart shape in the middle of the hook.

Tools and Materials

- STEEL RULER
- PENCIL
- BLANKET OR THICK CLOTH
- WORKBENCH
- BRADAWL
- CANDLE WAX OR SOAP
- D RINGS/SCREW EYES OR RINGS, GLASS PLATES
- PICTURE CORD OR WIRE
- SCISSORS
- WIRE CUTTERS
- SUITABLE WALL FIXING
- DRILL (OPTIONAL)

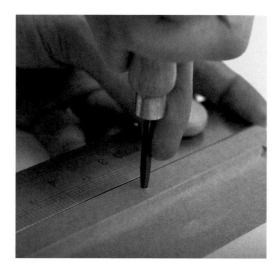

1 Measuring from the top of the frame, make a pencil mark a quarter of the way down both sides of the frame. Using the bradawl, make a small pilot hole at each of these points. Make sure you don't make the holes too near the edges. Also, if using a sloped molding, be sure to position the holes in the deepest part of the wood.

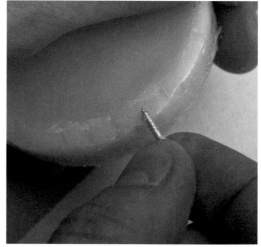

2 Place a little candle wax or soap onto the thread of the screw or screw ring, depending on what hanger you have decided to use. The wax or soap acts as a lubricant, makes the process easier, and prevents the screw eyes/rings from weakening or possibly breaking.

Choice of hangings

ON THE FRAME

   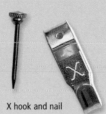

D ring   Screw eye   Screw ring

A D ring when used with a screw is a very strong hanging method and also does not stick out too much at the back of the frame.

A screw eye or a screw ring (a screw eye with a key ring on it) is just as functional but the pictures will hang at more of an angle from the wall because the screw rings/eyes protrude more. Screw rings are probably the cheapest option.

ON THE WALL

Double X hook and nails

X hook and nail

In most cases, an X hook or double X hook matched to the weight of the picture will be sufficient to hang it on a cavity or solid wall using a wall plug. If you have cavity walls, make sure you fix the hook into a stud or cross-brace.

GLASS PLATES

Heavy pictures can be screwed to the wall with glass plates that have been screwed to the frame. Be aware that the glass plate will show from the front of the frame.

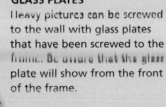

Glass plates are screwed into the back of the frame and into the wall.

PICTURE RAILS

There are specially designed picture rail hooks for use with picture rails. Simply attach cord, chain, or picture wire to the back of the picture as demonstrated on pages 68 and 70.

CORD OR WIRE?

You will need to attach picture cord or picture wire to the hangings. Both materials are very strong. The wire is just wrapped around itself whereas the cord is tied with a reef knot. If you are not very confident with knots, use picture wire.

Wire

Cord

CHAIN

An alternative to picture cord or wire is chain.

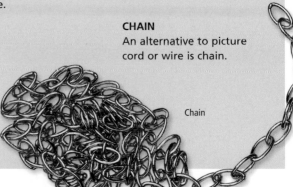

Chain

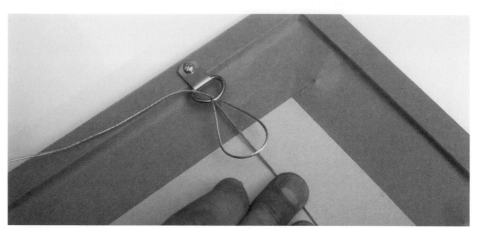

3 Screw D rings into each side of the frame.

4 If you are using picture wire: Cut off a length of wire twice the distance between the hangings. Loop the wire through the hangings with equal excess on each side. Then double loop the wire through the picture hanging and wrap it around itself into the middle of the frame.

Allow a little slack in the wire and do not make the wire too tight as the extra strain on the wire when hanging on the wall may in time pull the frame apart.

Alternative methods

Alternatively, you could screw screw rings into each side of the frame.

If you are using picture cord: Cut off a length about 8 inches (200mm) longer than twice the distance between the hangers. Thread the cord through each hanging and tie a reef knot to secure the cord.

10 rules for hanging pictures

1 Use candle wax on the threads of the screws to act as a lubricant to prevent the screw breaking when inserted.

2 Attach the hangings with D rings or screw eyes positioned a quarter of the way down the side of the frame.

3 Always make sure the hangings used are strong enough to take the weight of the frame.

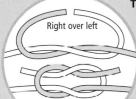

TO TIE A REEF KNOT
Right over left, and under; left over right and under.

Right over left

Left over right

4 Use only picture cord or picture wire, rather than garden twine or cotton thread as these will break.

5 If using nylon picture cord, tie the cord using a reef knot so that the knot is self-tightening

6 When using picture wire, double-loop the wire through the "D" ring or screw eye and then wrap it around itself to secure.

7 X hooks used with matching nails are the best hooks for use in softer walls, and larger X hooks combined with a suitable wall plug and screw are best used for hard walls.

8 Always test the strength of your chosen hangings by holding your picture by the wire or cord approximately 6 inches (150mm) from the floor.

9 Always select the position of the wall hook so that the picture will hang at eye-level.

10 To keep the picture away from the wall, use two slices of cork on the two bottom corners of the frame.

TO REDUCE GLARE
Hang pictures at a slightly tilted angle to reduce glare.

See also
Aesthetic decisions: *page 28*

Displaying pictures

There are no hard and fast rules about just where and how you should hang picture frames; the best rule of thumb is whether or not you like the finished results. However, there are guidelines you can follow regarding the grouping and arrangement.

Most pictures look best hung in groups to form a block rather than spaced out randomly over a large area. Unless a picture is fairly large, it is best not to hang it alone on the wall or it can look lost. The only exceptions are very large posters, prints, or ornate frames which are visually strong and imposing enough to make a statement by themselves.

Before you start to hammer picture nails in the wall, experiment with the layout by laying the framed images in groups on the floor. This will allow you to play around with sizes, shapes, and colors until you find a grouping you like. To work out the arrangement precisely, you can measure the wall space available and then mark out these boundaries on the floor with lengths of string.

CHOOSING THE WALL

Groups of pictures look best integrated as closely as possible with furnishings or any architectural features in a room. Use furniture as a guide for the outer vertical boundaries of your group. These might align with a sideboard or chest of drawers, for instance in which case you can imagine a rectangle "drawn" on the wall up from the edges of the piece of furniture. This same principle works for the space above a bed or behind a couch.

The way your walls are decorated will dictate which pictures look best on them. White or plain light-colored walls look best with clear strong colors and pictures displayed in simple frames without mats. Monochrome prints and photos also look very effective on light walls. For colored walls, it is a good idea either to echo the color scheme of the room in the picture mat or to use the mat as an effective contrast. If walls are painted in dark solid colors, the pictures may need light-colored mats.

Patterned walls need the most care, as the picture and the wall covering should not seem to be jostling with each other for attention. The color, size, and style of the wall-covering pattern will dictate the type of frame that looks best, but some sort of mat is almost always essential to give the picture clear definition.

INTEGRATE WITH FURNITURE
Positioned above a side table, this picture draws the eye down toward the table display.

PRACTICALITIES

While just about any flat vertical surface can become home to a picture frame, try not to hang pictures where they will be constantly knocked—in a narrow hall or close to the back of a chair—or you will be constantly having to straighten them.

Avoid hanging pictures above a radiator, as the rising heat, together with dust and grease carried upward, can damage the picture and may crack the glue of the frame. In general, pictures should not be hung in direct sunlight or opposite a window, especially if they are valuable. Watercolors are particularly vulnerable as they fade easily. In addition, if the picture is glazed, the reflection of the window can make it difficult to see the image.

The lamps appear to border the picture.

The eye is drawn down to the arrangement on the table.

BUILDING A SHAPE

When hanging groups of pictures it's best to plan out how you will hang them before you start hammering in nails.

THIRDS

A group of pictures will look best if it does not appear to split obviously into either half or quarters. Groups that fall naturally into thirds tend to be more harmonious. Hang the central picture—the most eye-catching and interesting—at eye-level when standing or when seated; the latter could be effective in a dining room, for instance. As a rule, larger pictures look best when placed at the bottom of a group; otherwise, the arrangement can look top-heavy.

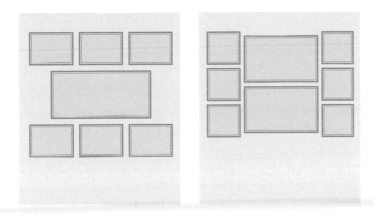

The grouping divides into thirds with smaller pieces on the outer edges.

Larger frames are kept to the center for balance.

The grouping is aligned with the couch.

THIRDS

In this symmetrical grouping of pictures, the tops of the smaller frames on the outside are aligned to give the grouping unity.

FORMAL GROUPINGS

There are two basic types of grouping: geometric and informal. For the former, the pictures can be hung in a straight line or arranged in a neat square or rectangle. Formal geometric groups work best when the frame moldings are identical and the pictures the same shape and size. This style works well with modern furnishings and is a good way to display a set of matching prints or photographs.

FORMAL GROUPING

A formal arrangement has a structured appearance here, aligned with the bed, the main feature of the room.

The frames are all of the same size and style.

GEOMETRIC ARRANGEMENT

A geometric picture arrangement can be used either to emphasize or to play down the proportions of a room. A long horizontal line of pictures will have the effect of lessening the height of a tall, lofty ceiling, while a tall column of pictures takes the eye up and makes a room with a low ceiling seem taller and more spacious.

INFORMAL ARRANGEMENT

For pictures of different sizes, shapes, and types, you will need an informal arrangement. Be prepared to experiment to find the most pleasing distribution of shapes—it may help to imagine the outline of the group forming a rectangle, circle, or triangle. Generally, large pictures look best with fairly wide gaps between them, while smaller pictures need to be hung closer together to avoid a sparse appearance.

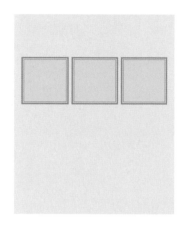
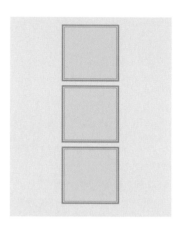

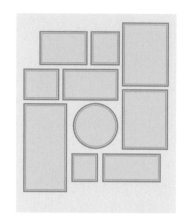

The pictures are aligned at the top for a sense of unity.

The gaps between the pictures are adjusted according to the sizes of the frames.

The arrangement forms a focal point above the couch.

INFORMAL ARRANGEMENT
An eclectic mix of frames in different sizes fills this wall.

LIGHTING

Not all pictures look best when strongly lit. You may wish to highlight the central frame in a group or highlight just one or two smaller frames. Apart from natural daylight, there are basically two ways to light pictures: either by spotlighting (positioning an ordinary light or spotlight to shine onto the room) or by fixing a light on or near the frame itself. Experiment using the types of lamp mentioned below until you find exactly the effect you want.

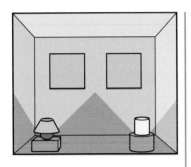

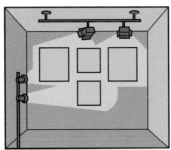

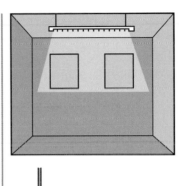

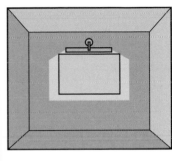

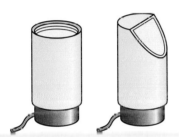

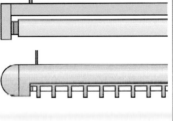

UPLIGHTS

Uplights give an even, diffused light. They can be positioned on the table, on the floor directly under the frames, or hidden among foliage or behind a chair.

SPOTLIGHTS

Spotlights can be adjusted to create direct or reflected light. Low-voltage tungsten-halogen spotlights are small and discreet, and can be used as ceiling lights, as individual wall-spots, or in a standard-style floor fitting; two or more individual spots can be mounted on a strip track attached to the wall or ceiling.

STRIPS

A fluorescent strip will light a complete group of pictures. A good technique to use in a large room is to fit a diffuser to angle to light onto the pictures and choose a "daylight" colored bulb for the most natural effect.

PICTURE LIGHTS

Picture lights are individual units attached directly to the picture or the wall just above it. They are available in a range of modern and traditional styles, so can be chosen to match both your room and the picture. Make sure the fitting is wide enough to light the whole picture—it should be about two-thirds of the picture's width. If it throws a reflection on the glass or varnish, you can reduce it simply by tilting the picture slightly toward the floor.

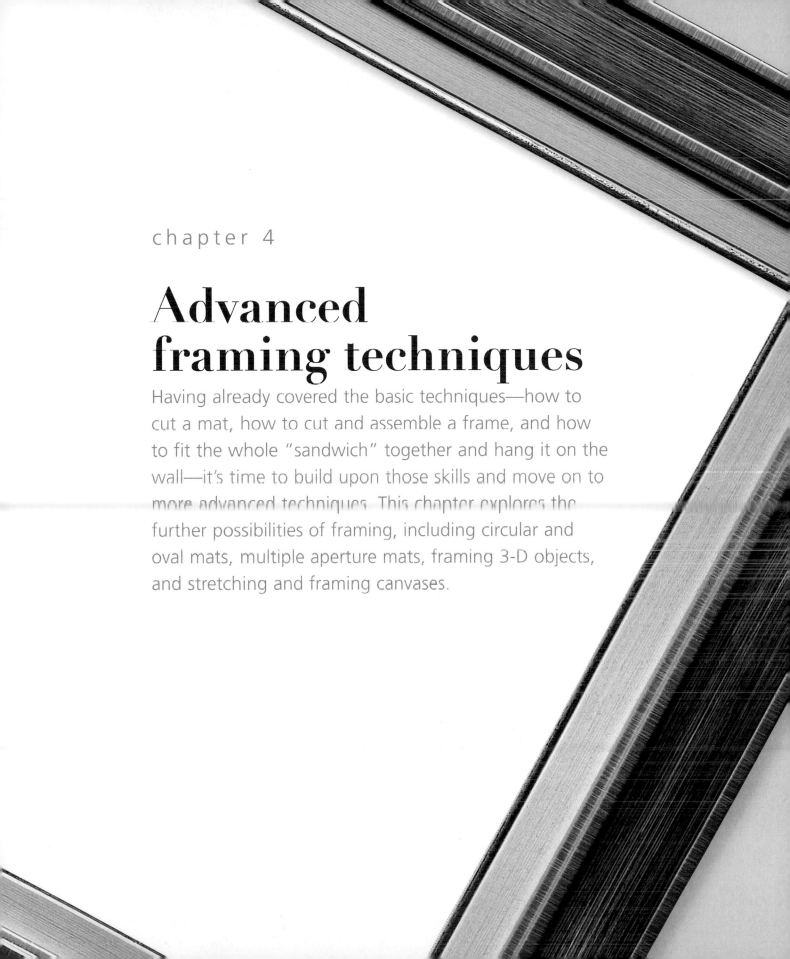

chapter 4

Advanced framing techniques

Having already covered the basic techniques—how to cut a mat, how to cut and assemble a frame, and how to fit the whole "sandwich" together and hang it on the wall—it's time to build upon those skills and move on to more advanced techniques. This chapter explores the further possibilities of framing, including circular and oval mats, multiple aperture mats, framing 3-D objects, and stretching and framing canvases.

See also
Aesthetic decisions: *page 28*
Mat cutting: *page 38*

Double or slip mats

A double, or slip, mat is often used when matting a picture to add depth and a third dimension, and helps lead the viewer's eye into the image. The inner mat can be used to draw attention to one key area of color in the picture; this also has the effect of toning down other areas of the image.

Double mats are usually designed so that the inner color is darker than the outer color. Notice here how the use of a darker, sepia color emphasizes the dark outline of this world map.

Mat width
The width of the inner mat is usually ¼ inch (6mm) but it can be any width that you think looks appropriate. A wider inner mat can look very effective and also has the advantage of disguising any uneven cutting. A narrower ¼ inch (6mm) inner mat would be more likely to show any errors in cutting.

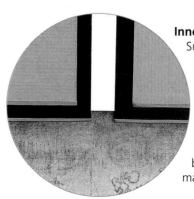

Inner mats
Subtle changes in the tone of matboard can have quite extreme outcomes on the finished picture. The samples here have only slightly different colored inner mats but the effects are very noticeable. Always blend the tone of the materials to the picture.

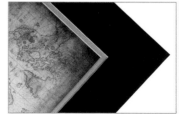 

Outer mats
A darker outer mat and a lighter inner mat combination can be used, but make sure that the darker outer mat does not dominate the picture. As with inner mats, slightly different colors can make a big difference.

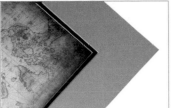

Red inner mat

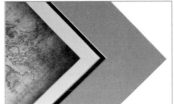

Red outer mat

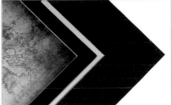

White inner border **Triple mat with white inner border**

Brightly colored mats

Be careful when using brightly colored inner mats, such as red ones, because the viewer's eye may be drawn to the picture framing and not the picture. This is also applies if a red matboard is used for the outer board because this can easily dominate the image. However, this choice could be appropriate if you are matching the frame to the décor.

Triple mats

Triple mats can be used to good effect to highlight key color areas or important features of your pictures. The differences in widths can have very different effects, so experiment with several different samples of matboard. You can also use a triple mat to create a white inner border. If you are framing your own work, you can use a white innermost border to add your signature.

Tools and Materials

- **STEEL RULER: 24 INCH (60CM)**
- **YOUR CHOSEN PICTURE**
- **PENCIL WITH #2 LEAD OR HARDER**
- **ERASER**
- **SCRAP PAPER**
- **YOUR TWO CHOSEN COLORS OF MATBOARD**
- **SELF-HEALING CUTTING MAT**
- **UTILITY KNIFE**
- **ADHESIVE PUTTY**
- **MAT CUTTER**
- **RAZOR BLADE**
- **GLUE STICK**

Cutting double mats

1 Measure the picture to be matted and make a note of the size. Make a rough sketch of the mats to be cut on a piece of scrap paper, and this will help to eliminate measuring mistakes.

2 Using the same size borders for both mats, add dimensions for the inside size of the picture to the first mat. Once you have established the outside size, mark out your first mat's outside size. This mat will form the inner mat.

Calculating border widths

In the diagram below, the picture shown has an actual size of 10 x 8 inches (254 x 200mm). The inside size will measure 9¾ x 7¾ inches (248 x 194mm). The inner mat will have borders of 2½ inches (62mm) and there will be ¼ inch (6mm) of the inner mat showing. This means the outer mat will have borders of 2¼ inches (56mm) to allow the inner mat to show.

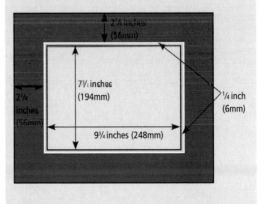

Tip

If signing your work it may look better to make the base of the inner border much wider than the top and side inner borders.

3 Place the mat on a self-healing cutting mat. Secure the ruler in place with some adhesive putty and use the utility knife and ruler to cut out the outside size of the mat. Remember when cutting to keep the knife at as low an angle as possible in relation to the board.

4 Mark out the borders on the back of the matboard. In this case they are 2½ inches (62mm).

5 When the inside size is marked out, double check this measurement with a ruler. As a final check, place the picture over the inside size you have just marked out. If you can just see the eight guidelines in the corners of the picture, the mat will fit when cut.

6 Cut out the aperture of the inner mat using your chosen mat cutter. For further guidance on mat cutting, see pages 38–41. Don't push out the inside piece of matboard if it is still just attached at the corners; carefully use a razor blade to finish off the cut.

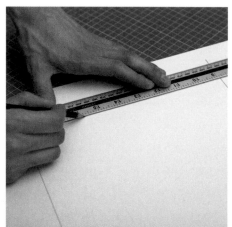

7 Now mark out the outer mat. Care should be taken to ensure that both pieces of matboard are exactly the same size. Make the border widths on the second outer mat ¼ inch (6mm) narrower than the inner mat you have already cut. This will allow ¼ inch (6mm) of the inner mat to be visible. Also make sure your markings are visible to make the job easier when you come to cut the apertures. Using a mat cutter, cut out the aperture of the outer mat.

Narrow inner mats

The visible area of an inner mat is usually ¼ inch (6mm), however, interesting effects can be created with very narrow inner mounts. Unfortunately the narrower the inner mat the harder it is to measure and cut evenly, so plenty of practice is needed before reducing the width of the inner mat below ¼ inch (6mm).

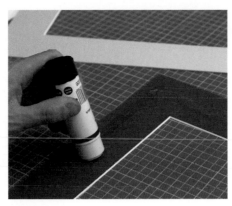

8 Once the two mats are cut, place the outer mat over the inner mat to check for correct sizing and evenness of inner borders. Smooth down any burrs on the bevels with your thumb.

9 The mats are stuck together using a glue stick. This allows for repositioning if they are initially placed out of alignment. Apply an even coat of glue around the borders of the inner mat. Use plenty of glue; about two to three sweeps up and down each side will ensure adhesion. Don't put glue on the outer mat surface as this will ruin your mat. When applying the glue to the inner mat be sure not to get too near to the beveled edge as the glue will show.

10 Align the outer mat over the top of the glued inner mat and press into the correct position.

11 Use your fist to burnish the two pieces of mat together. This should be left to dry for at least an hour. The two mats can be weighted down to ensure adhesion but be careful not to dent the matboard.

Deeper mat base

If more mat is desired at the base of the mat, trim down ¼ inch (6mm) from the top and sides of the mat.

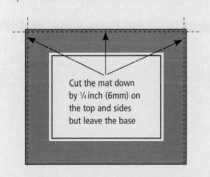

Cut the mat down by ¼ inch (6mm) on the top and sides but leave the base

Hinge the picture to the double mat and it should look like this.

See also
Aesthetic decisions: *page 28*
Mat cutting: *page 38*

Multiple aperture mats

Sometimes you may want to frame more than one picture in a single frame. The images could be a selection of family photographs, for example. Or you could have a main picture with a central theme and several pictures around it. Alternatively you could have a main picture and then an extra aperture for information, including the place/date/artist, etc. Unless you're a calligrapher, this information can be typed and printed on a home computer (be sure to choose a font sympathetic with the images being displayed). The easiest way to achieve this is to use a multiple aperture mat.

One image is divided into three for the multiple aperture mat.

Tools and Materials

- **STEEL RULER: 24 INCH (60CM)**
- **PENCIL WITH #2 LEAD OR HARDER**
- **ERASER**
- **SCRAP PAPER**
- **YOUR CHOSEN COLOR(S) OF MATBOARD**
- **SELF-HEALING CUTTING MAT**
- **UTILITY KNIFE OR CRAFT KNIFE**
- **ADHESIVE PUTTY**
- **MAT CUTTER**
- **RAZOR BLADE**
- **MASKING TAPE**

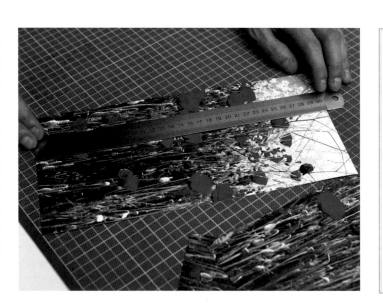

1 Measure the pictures to be matted and make a note of the individual sizes. Make a rough sketch of the different size apertures on a scrap piece of paper, this will help to avoid measuring mistakes.

Tip

If you are not very confident about your math skills get a friend to check your work. If you want to avoid the math you don't have to cut down your matboard to the exact outside size; work with a larger piece instead and cut down the borders after cutting out the apertures.

Choosing a color for a multiple aperture mat

As with all picture framing projects, the choice of materials is important, but they should be given special consideration when creating a multiple aperture mat because the pictures included could be quite varied. Here, we are focusing on mat color but the same careful consideration should be paid to the frame.

Here we have three photographs of flowers in a field. The first mat color that may be suitable is cream. The rich color of the flowers is complemented by the warmth of the cream border and it seems a good choice. A good rule for choosing a matboard color is, "If in doubt, choose cream."

The flowerheads are a reddish tone so a red color could help to emphasize this feature. However, this choice of materials could overpower the subtleness of the pictures, so be careful.

Black can provide a very powerful background to any photograph (especially black and white photographs).

Neutral colors can work well with your multiple aperture projects and could be a good choice if there are no uniting colors in each picture. This gray tone is a good compromise.

The stems of the flowers are green, so the use of a green matboard could be effective. However, care should be taken to pick the right tone of green to suit the pictures. Green can become overpowering if it is too bright or luminous in tone.

Bar widths

If the bars between the pictures on a multiple mat are too wide, the pictures can appear to be unrelated. Ideally, they should be a lot narrower than the outer borders of the mat. A good guideline measurement to use is ¾–1 inch (20–25mm).

Tip

Building on the theme of double mats, you could use color to create a third dimension to your multiple aperture projects. However, do not get too carried away with design ideas as this could distract the viewer's eye.

Sketch the mat

Work out the outside size of the multiple aperture mat. For this example three photographs with an actual size of 12 x 6 inches (300 x 150mm) have been used. Therefore the inside size measures 11¾ x 5¾ inches (294 x 145mm).
To obtain the outside size add together:
2½ + 5¾ +¾ + 5¾ +¾ + 5¾ + 2½ = 23¾ inches (62 + 145 + 15 +145 +15 +145 + 62 = 589mm)

2½ + 11¾ + 2¾ (more mat at base) = 17 inches (62 + 194 + 68 = 324mm)
Remember to add the extra ¼ inch (6mm) at the base of the mat.
Therefore the outside size in this case = 23¾ x 17 inches (589 x 324mm). You can now cut out your outside size of the matboard.

2 Place the mat on the self-healing cutting mat. On the back of the matboard, mark the desired measurements for the outside size of the mat with a pencil. Secure the ruler in place using adhesive putty and cut out the outside size of the mat using the utility knife.

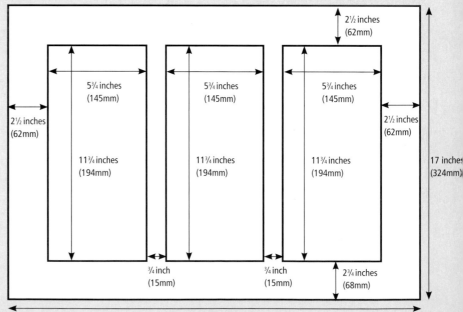

2½ inches (62mm)

5¾ inches (145mm)   5¾ inches (145mm)   5¾ inches (145mm)

2½ inches (62mm)   2½ inches (62mm)

11¾ inches (194mm)   11¾ inches (194mm)   11¾ inches (194mm)

17 inches (324mm)

¾ inch (15mm)   ¾ inch (15mm)   2¾ inches (68mm)

23¾ inches (589mm)

3 To mark out, start at one side of the matboard and work across to the other side. So for the example used, mark out 2½ inches (62mm), then 5¾ inches (145mm), then ¾ inch (15mm) and so on. Join up these lines with a pencil and ruler.

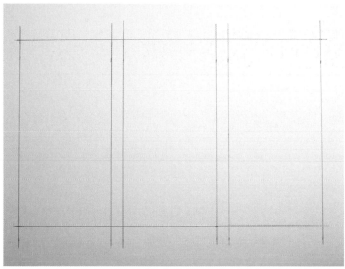

4 Next, mark down the desired measurements from the top of the matboard. Join up these additional lines with a pencil and ruler. The matboard is now marked out ready to cut.

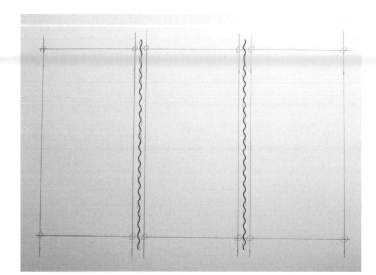

5 It can be easy to make a mistake when cutting out the apertures. It can also be difficult to know where to start and stop each cut. Additional markings on the back of the matboard can help clarify the cutting process for you. Try adding a wiggly line to the narrow borders between pictures to make it more obvious which areas represent borders and which areas represent apertures. Also, adding a circle around each start and stop point can help avoid overcuts and possibly ruining the mat.

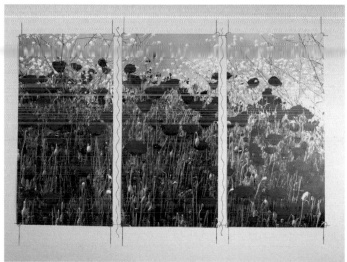

6 The apertures are now ready to cut out and your matboard should look like this. Be sure to measure each aperture to check it is the correct size. You can also position each picture over each aperture as a final check.

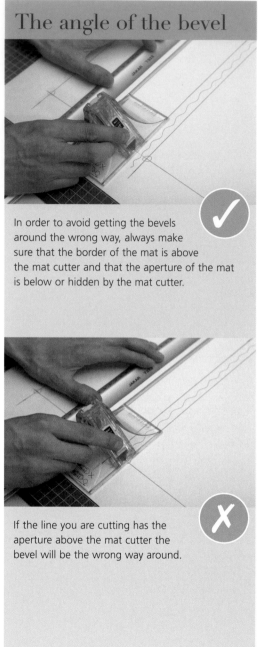

The angle of the bevel

In order to avoid getting the bevels around the wrong way, always make sure that the border of the mat is above the mat cutter and that the aperture of the mat is below or hidden by the mat cutter.

If the line you are cutting has the aperture above the mat cutter the bevel will be the wrong way around.

7 Use the mat cutter to cut out the apertures. If you have evenly sized pictures—as in this example—it is recommended that you cut each set of parallel lines in one "sweep." However, do remember to stop for each border. It sometimes helps to rehearse mentally where you are going to start and stop each cut.

8 Use a razor blade to remove each aperture on the final set of cuts. Remember to smooth down any rough edges on the bevels with an emery board.

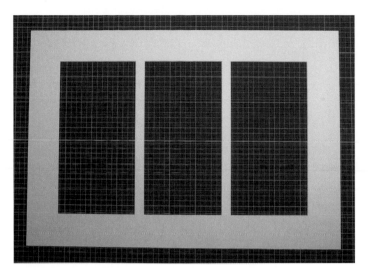

9 The mat should now be cut out and ready to attach your pictures.

10 Tape your pictures to the back of the overmat. Remember to hinge the photos if they are not already mounted onto thicker cardstock.

The multiple aperture mat is now ready to frame.

See also
Mat cutting: *page 38*
Glass cutting: *page 56*

Oval and circular mats

By using an oval or circular aperture on a picture, certain areas that are not of interest at the corners can be cropped. Such applications for oval/circular mats can be used for single portraits of people and for images with an off-center focal point. To cut an oval or circular mat it is necessary to buy a mat cutter specifically designed for the purpose.

Oval/circle mat cutter.

Tools and Materials

- **STEEL RULER**
- **PENCIL**
- **ERASER**
- **SCRAP PAPER**
- **YOUR CHOICE OF MATBOARD**
- **SELF-HEALING CUTTING MAT**
- **LARGE PIECE OF SCRAP MATBOARD**
- **UTILITY KNIFE**
- **MASKING TAPE**
- **PURPOSE-MADE OVAL/ CIRCULAR MAT CUTTER**
- **MALLET (OPTIONAL)**

Cutting oval mats

If you're a novice, work with smaller pictures to begin with. A good place to start is a 6 x 4–inch (150 x 100mm) photograph. Purpose-made oval mat cutters are also recommended as they provide a more even and accurate 45-degree bevel when compared to a mat cut with a knife and ruler.

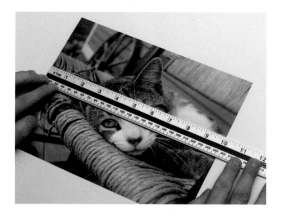

1 Measure the picture to be matted and make a sketch of the oval mat. Take into account that you will be covering a large amount of the picture in the corners. Make sure that you don't cover the artist's signature if this is important.

Sketch the mat

The picture used here has an actual size of 10 x 8 inches (250 x 200mm), so the inside size will be 9¾ x 7¾ inches (244 x 194mm). The borders will be 1½ inches (38mm) on the top and sides with 1¾ inches (44mm) on the base. Smaller borders tend to be used on ovals and circles.
To obtain the outside size add together:
9¾ + 1½ + 1½ = 12¾ inches
(244 + 38 + 38 = 320mm)
7¾ + 1½ + 1¾ = 11 inches
(194 + 38 + 44 = 276mm)
Therefore the outside size in this case = 12¾ x 11 inches (320 x 276mm).

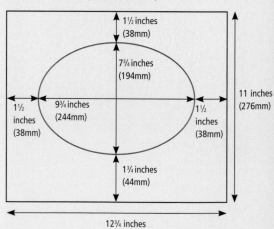

1½ inches (38mm)

7¾ inches (194mm)

1½ inches (38mm)   9¾ inches (244mm)   1½ inches (38mm)

11 inches (276mm)

1¾ inches (44mm)

12¾ inches (320mm)

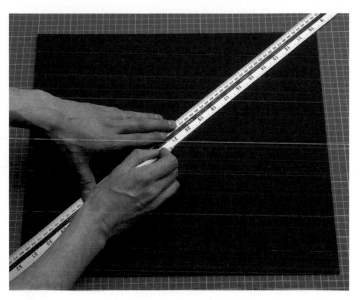

2 After establishing the outside size, cut a piece of matboard at least 4 inches (100mm) larger than the outside size. In this case the board measures 17 x 15 inches (420 x 376mm) This is to allow for any inaccuracies when marking out the center of the matboard.

3 Find the center of your matboard by lining up the ruler with two diagonally opposite corners. Then make a small line about 4 inches (100mm) long in the middle of the board. Repeat this for the opposite two corners. Where the two lines intersect is the exact center of your matboard.

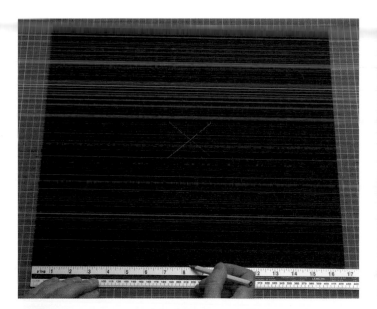

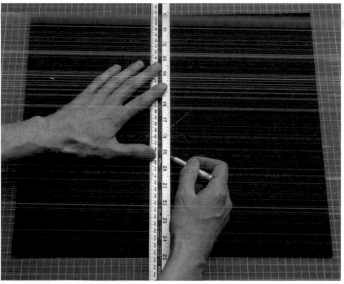

4 Now measure the distance from the outside edge of the board to the center of the cross you have marked out. This should be half of the length of the board, in this case 8½ inches (210mm). Mark the long side of the matboard to this measurement.

5 Line up your ruler with the mark on the long side of the board and the center of the cross. Draw a line approximately 4 inches (100mm) long—2 inches (50mm) each side of the cross. Repeat this process for the short side of the matboard to create a total of four intersecting lines in the center of the matboard.

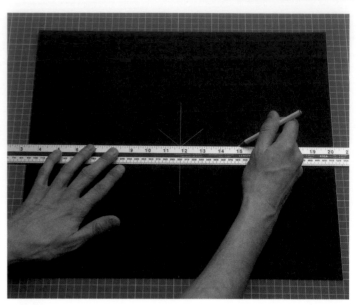

6 Now measure the distance from the short side of the board to the center of the diagonal cross. This should be half of the width of the board, in this case 7½ inches (188mm). Now mark this point.

7 Repeat this for the other side to create a total of four lines in the center of the mat board. You will use these lines to position the body of the oval mount cutter correctly.

Setting up the oval mat cutter

The oval mat cutter has two adjustable settings. One is set to the smallest dimension of the oval. The other is the "difference" between the two dimensions of the oval. The two different sizes of an oval are often referred to as the "major" and "minor" axes and you will need to subtract the minor axis, or the smallest dimension, from the major axis, or largest dimension, in order to set up the mat cutter accurately.

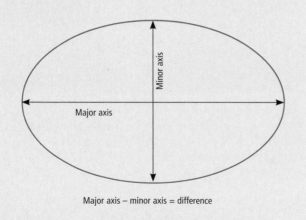

Major axis – minor axis = difference

8 The oval mat cutter can cut very deeply into your cutting mat and leave a permanent mark, so it's a good idea to attach a piece of scrap matboard—roughly the same size as your matboard—to your cutting mat. This is used as an extra "cutting mat." Secure the scrap matboard to the cutting mat with some masking tape.

9 Secure the marked-up matboard to the scrap and cutting mat with masking tape.

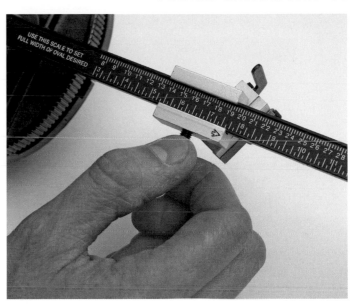

10 Set the measurements on the oval mat cutter. For this example the smallest dimension (minor axis) is 7¾ inches (194mm) so set the mat cutter arm to this measurement.

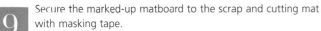

11 The difference between the two oval measurements (width and height of the picture) is 2 inches (50mm), so the middle setting on the oval mat cutter needs to be set to 2 inches (50mm).

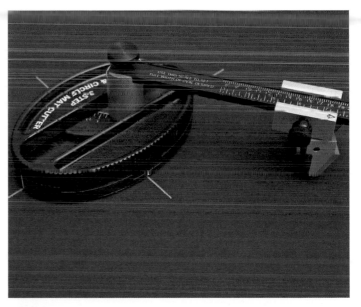

12 The oval mat cutter is positioned on the mat by aligning the four white marks on its outer rim with the four 4–inch (100mm) center marks that you made on your matboard in steps 5–7.

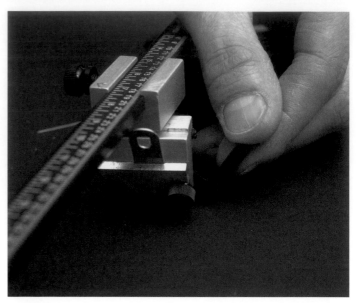

13 Secure the mat cutter in position using the four metal points protruding from its base. In order for the mat cutter to stay in the same place pressure may need to be applied to it. You could lightly tap the base of the mat cutter with a mallet to improve adhesion.

14 The oval mat cutter used here works by slowly lowering the blade depth so that the oval bevel is cut into the matboard a little at a time. The blade depth is adjusted with a lever at the side of the blade. The nearer the lever is to the blade, the deeper the cut. It has four distinct positions that click into place as you move the lever. To start, ensure the blade depth is at the shallowest setting. Do this by pushing the lever as far as possible from the blade.

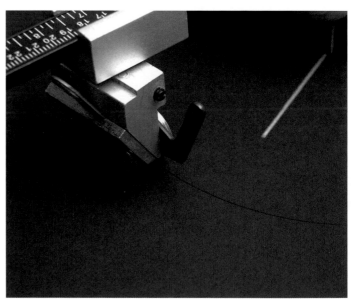

15 With the cutter blade at the shallowest depth swing the mat cutter arm around two complete turns. This allows the blade to find the true elliptical path. You may need to change hands on the swing arm of the mat cutter to try to keep an even pressure.

16 Now move the blade depth down by one click and move the swing arm around again. The blade should need at least three complete turns to allow the blade to cut through the matboard. Repeat for the remaining two clicks of the mat cutter blade.

17 You should make at least three complete turns with the mat cutter to allow the blade to gently cut through the matboard.

18 When the blade is set at the deepest and you have made at least three complete turns with the cutter, gently lift the center away. If it will not completely release, try another sweep of the cutter with more downward pressure. For safety, once the middle of the mat is removed, make sure you return the blade in the mat cutter to the shallowest depth.

Check what your mat looks like on your picture.

A circular mat will suit this image because the focal point is slightly off-center.

Cutting circular mats

The techniques used to cut oval mats are also used for circular mats, but with one key difference: when cutting circular mats there are no minor and major dimensions, and therefore no "difference" to calculate because you're dealing with a perfectly round circle.

For this example a 10 x 8–inch (254 x 200mm) photograph of a sailing scene has been used. The focal point of the photograph is not quite centrally positioned in the image; a circular aperture in a mat can correct this. An off-white matboard has been chosen to emphasize the warm tones present in the image.

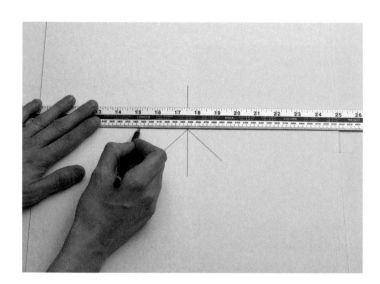

1 Measure your picture. In this case the actual size is 10 x 8 inches (254 x 200mm) so the inside size can be no larger than a circle with a 7¾-inch (194mm) diameter. Cut the outside size of the board so that it measures at least 4 inches (100mm) bigger than the actual size of the picture. Then find the center of the matboard, and mark out the four lines to align your oval mat cutter to (see page 90).

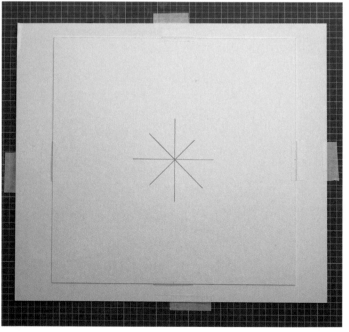

2 Secure a piece of scrap matboard to your cutting mat and then attach your marked up mat to the scrap.

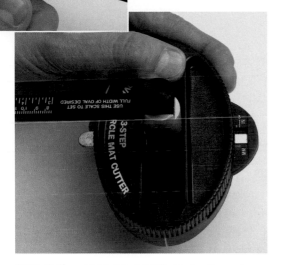

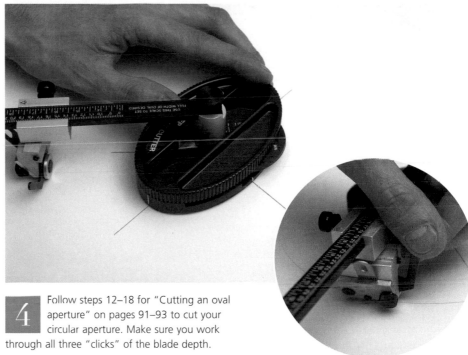

3 The measurement on the mat cutter swing arm is set to 7¾ inches (194mm), the diameter of the circle, and because there is no "difference" (see page 90) the setting on the mat cutter center is set to zero.

4 Follow steps 12–18 for "Cutting an oval aperture" on pages 91–93 to cut your circular aperture. Make sure you work through all three "clicks" of the blade depth.

5 Gently lift away the middle of the aperture, making sure that the cutter has cut all the way through the matboard. For safety, once the middle of the mat is removed, make sure you return the blade in the mat cutter to the shallowest depth.

The finished mat on the picture.

See also
Frame assembly: *page 52*
Framing needlework: *page 102*

Framing 3-D art

There are several ways of framing 3-D art. "3-D art" means anything that has a raised surface that the glass will need to be kept away from. Items you might want to frame include medals, coins, buttons, badges, needlework with beads, deeds with wax seals, papier-mâché works of art (such as face masks), items of clothing (signed sport shirts for example), and
even wedding dresses.

Decorative buttons can be displayed in a box frame.

Using a wooden fillet

The main point to consider when framing 3-D artwork is how best to keep the glass away from the picture. Glass should be used to keep the item and the matboard clean. You can frame without glass but it is not recommended.

A suitably deep molding needs to be used when framing 3-D art. Box frame moldings are available in varying depths and finishes but you need to make sure there will be enough room for the glass, the picture to be framed, and the backing.

The easiest way to keep the glass away from the work of art is to use a wooden fillet. Take care to choose a fillet shallower than the rabbet of your molding or it will show from the front when

framed. The cutting, or mitering, of the fillet needs to be accurate but using a fillet is a simple and speedy technique to use.

Using double-thickness matboard

Another very effective way to keep the glass away from the artwork is to use double-thickness matboard that's the same color as the matboard used to mat the artwork. This creates real depth to your work and is more visually impressive than a simple plain wood fillet because the box frame appears to be lined with the same color all around.

Box frame molding

Wooden fillets

Framing a 3-D object

This demonstration shows how to construct a frame for a selection of buttons using double-thickness matboard as a fillet instead of wood.

Tools and Materials

- STEEL RULER
- BOX FRAME MOLDING
- SUITABLE COLOR OF MATBOARD
- GLUES: CRAFT GLUE, WOOD GLUE, EPOXY GLUE
- UTILITY KNIFE
- SELF-HEALING CUTTING MAT
- ADHESIVE PUTTY
- CHAMOIS
- COTTON CLOTH
- SMALL BRUSH
- NAILS
- SMALL HAMMER

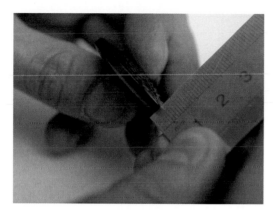

1 Measure your 3-D art to establish its maximum height. You will need to know this in order to know how deep your fillet needs to be to keep the glass from touching the artwork.

2 Choose your frame and matboard materials. Make sure the molding is deep enough to allow everything—glass, 3-D artwork, matboard, and backing—to fit into the frame.

Deepening a frame with wooden batten

If you have become quite confident with frame assembly, you can make your frames as deep as you need by using a wooden batten secured to the back of the frame. This will provide you with very deep boxes but you will need to finish off the untreated wood with a suitable stain or paint to match the top frame.

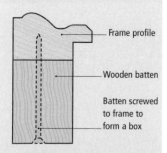

Frame profile

Wooden batten

Batten screwed to frame to form a box

3 The buttons to be framed vary in color. Therefore a neutral white matboard and a plain ash molding for the frame have been selected. When choosing your matboard be careful that the 3-D art will not be lost in the background.

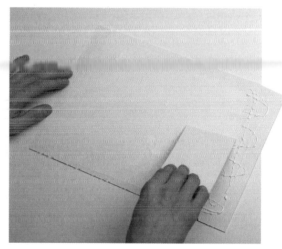

4 Construct a double-thickness piece of matboard by gluing two pieces of matboard together. The pieces of matboard should measure at least 3 inches (75mm) longer than the largest dimension of your finished frame size. Apply glue liberally to one piece of matboard. Spread it around so that it forms an even coat.

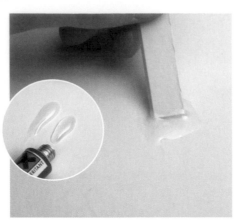

Conservation

5 Carefully position the two pieces of matboard together, being careful of any overspill at the edges. Once these two pieces of matboard are aligned correctly, leave the glue to dry. You could weight them down while they dry if you like.

6 Secure the work of art to the matboard. This can be achieved in two ways: either stitch the buttons onto the board or glue them. If it is a non-valuable artwork, you may want to use an epoxy glue. Because there is no particular value to the buttons they will be glued.

When deciding which attachment method to use you must consider the value of the artwork. For anything of value, such as medals, coins, etc., it is recommended that you use a technique that can easily be reversed. This is called "conservation framing" and is very important for the preservation of artwork. Medals can easily be stitched to matboard. Coins can have cutouts made for them. Most items can be stitched but a pilot hole may be needed. If the item is too heavy to be stitched, you can frame it so that its weight is supported by the bottom of the frame.

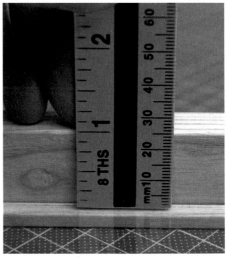

7 Glue the artwork to the matboard. Take care not to apply too much glue to avoid the glue showing when viewed from the front. Allow time for the glue to dry before fitting the artwork into the frame.

8 Once the outside size has been decided, make the frame. You could also use an overmat to help keep the glass away from your 3-D artwork. Once these tasks are completed, again, check the depth of the highest point of the 3-D artwork to determine exactly how deep to make your fillet.

9 The depth of the deepest button is ½ inch (12mm). Therefore a depth of ¾ inch (20mm) was used for the fillet, but be sure to check the depth of the frame after the glass is added to ensure you have enough room.

10 Using the double-thickness matboard you prepared earlier, mark out four strips for the fillet.

11 Cut the strips out using the knife and steel ruler, working on a cutting mat. Be sure to secure the ruler in place with adhesive putty and keep the knife angle as low as possible to the matboard.

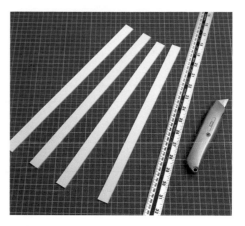

12 You should have four strips of double-thickness matboard to be used as fillets in your box frame.

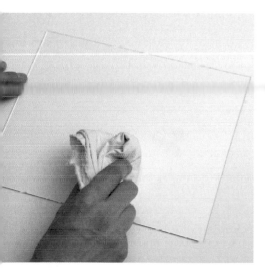

13 Clean the glass of the box frame with a wet chamois and then a dry cotton cloth.

14 Place the glass into the box frame and then measure the length of what will be the top of the frame when it hangs on the wall. This is for the first fillet. When measuring the length of the fillets be sure to make them a tight fit.

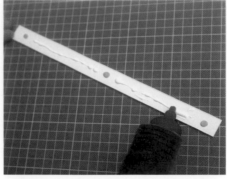

Tip

The combination of adhesive putty and glue is used so that the adhesive putty holds the fillet in place until the glue has dried. Make sure the pieces of adhesive putty are very small so that they do not form an uneven surface along the fillet. Position the fillet at the top first, and then at the bottom. Position the side fillets last as these help to keep the top fillet in place while the glue dries.

15 Mark out this length on one of your four pieces of double-thickness matboard. Position the ruler along the fillet so that the straight end of the ruler is on your measuring mark and you can use the end of the ruler to cut along. Check for accuracy after cutting. If it is slightly too long make sure that you cut a small amount off so that the fillet does not have to be forced into position as this may cause it to bow and fall out later.

16 Use a combination of three very small pieces of adhesive putty and wood or craft glue to secure the fillet along the inside edge of the box frame. Apply three small pieces of adhesive putty along the fillet, one piece in the middle and the other two at each end. Apply the glue in between the adhesive putty.

17 Carefully position the fillet along the inside top edge of the box frame. Make sure the fillet is touching the glass before you push it against the frame to ensure an even and level fillet to rest your picture against.

18 Repeat this for the bottom fillet. Now measure the distance between the two pieces of fillet you have already glued into position to establish the correct length for the two remaining pieces of fillet.

19 Cut your two remaining pieces of fillet to this length and secure in position as before with glue and adhesive putty.

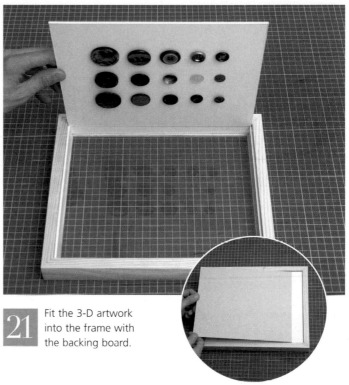

20 Once the glue has dried, remove any unsightly dust from the inside of the glass and the visible edges of the fillet with a clean brush.

21 Fit the 3-D artwork into the frame with the backing board.

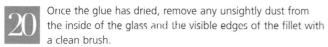

22 Initially use just two nails to secure the picture in the frame. Then check that the picture is dust free before finally fitting with the remaining nails. Finish off by tidying up the back of the frame with gummed paper tape.

The finished result is a real 3-D effect for your pictures.

See also
Framing 3-D art: *page 96*

Framing needlework

All kinds of needlework—embroidery, cross-stitch, tapestry, and lacework—require special treatment in order to be framed successfully. Before framing, they will need to be stretched over a suitable piece of board using thread to keep the fabric flat and taut.

An example of needlework.

Tools and Materials

- **YOUR CHOSEN NEEDLEWORK**
- **RULER**
- **CONSERVATION-QUALITY MATBOARD OR FOAM-CORE BOARD**
- **PINS**
- **HEAVY-DUTY THREAD**
- **TAPESTRY NEEDLE**
- **SCISSORS**

1 The example used here is a counted cross-stitch needlework sewn onto a light sand-colored fabric. Measure the size of the design on the needlework.

2 Decide how much of the fabric border you would like to show. For this particular example the needlework has plenty of fabric border to work with, so a generous border of 1½ inches (40mm) was chosen. This may not always be possible because needleworks are often sewn on smaller pieces of fabric. It may also be the case that your needlework has a distinct border as part of the design. Once you have decided what will become the inside size of the mat, add 1 inch (25mm) to this measurement. This will allow for positioning of the needlework on the board it is to be stretched over. Mark out and cut a piece of matboard over which the needlework can be stretched.

Conservation matboard

Conservation of artworks is important for all picture framing. Therefore it is recommended that you choose a piece of high quality matboard to stretch your needlework over. Higher quality matboard is called "acid free" or "neutral pH." It is more expensive but the lower levels of acid in the board will help to preserve the artwork. When choosing your matboard also be aware that the color of the board may show through the fabric so choose a board that matches the color of the fabric.

Using an overmat?

You will need to decide if you are going to overmat your needlework. As a general rule they are usually matted, in order to keep the glass away from the stitchwork and to prevent the stitches from becoming crushed. In addition, the choice of mats can be used to complement certain areas of the needlework. However, if you decide not to use an overmat you can always cut an invisible fillet from matboard to go between the glass and the stretched needlework to keep the glass away.

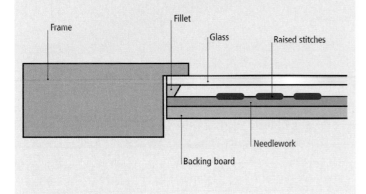

Frame — Fillet — Glass — Raised stitches — Needlework — Backing board

3 Check that your board is small enough to allow enough overlap of fabric to lace at the back. There should be at least ½ inch (12mm). Any less and the needlework may be pulled apart by the thread. You may need to stitch on extra fabric to allow secure stretching of your needlework at this stage.

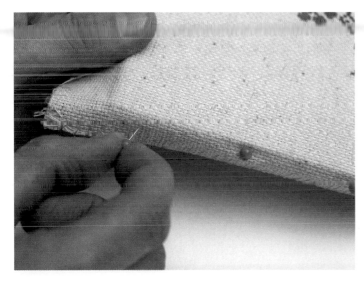

4 Position the needlework so that it is in the center of the board. Once this is done, pin the needlework in place. Start by pinning the needlework in the center of one side. Then place a pin in the center on the opposite side while pulling slightly on the fabric. This adds a little stretch to the needlework and will keep the needlework flat in the frame.

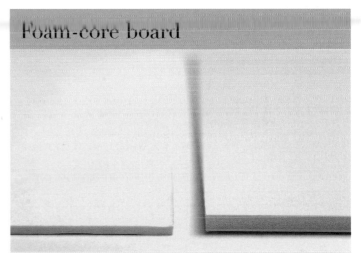

Foam-core board

The needlework can be pinned in place along the outer edge of the board before it is "laced" with thread. A good alternative to matboard is foam-core board, usually about ⅛–¼ inch (3–6mm) thick. This allows for easy pinning along the edge of the needlework but you will need a frame deep enough to cope with the extra depth created.

5 Continue to pin, working from the center of each side toward the edges and pulling the fabric taut each time you add a pin. The pins should be no further than 2 inches (50mm) apart. Ensure that the weave of the fabric is aligned straight along the edge of the board.

6 Cut a length of heavy-duty thread (such as upholstery thread) eight times the width of the needlework. Then thread a tapestry needle and pass needle and thread through the center of one edge of the fabric three times. It may also help to tie a knot to pull against.

Tip

It may be tempting to use self-adhesive tape to secure the needlework in place. Don't do it. The tape will dry out in six months' time and your needlework will buckle with changes in room temperature. Also, avoid self-adhesive boards because the impurities in the board will eventually stain your needlework.

7 Now begin "lacing" across the back of the needlework with the tapestry needle and thread, working from side to side and ensuring there is tension in the thread as you stitch. When you have fully laced two edges (you will need to re-thread the needle in order to complete this) remove the pins and see if the needlework remains stretched. If it does not you need to apply more tension when stitching.

8 Continue lacing until two sides of the needlework are stretched. Then repeat the technique for the other two sides.

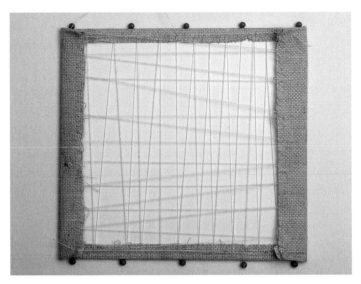

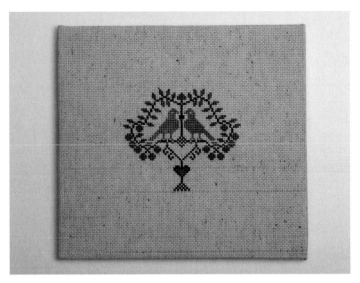

9 The back of the needlework should look like this when it is stretched. Cut off any loose threads so that they do not get in the way when matting and framing.

10 Remove the pins and check that the needlework remains stretched. If it has become uneven in places, add more stitching to ensure an even stretch.

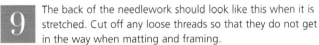

Alternative method

If there are any raised areas on the needlework, such as beads or buttons, it may be necessary to use a double mat. The extra thickness of the mat will keep the glass away from the needlework and also create a 3-D effect.

When framing needlework it is recommended that you use an inside size for the overmat that does not encroach on the stitches, so leave plenty of space around the design.

See also
Frame cutting using a miter saw: *page 48*
Frame assembly: *page 52*

Framing art on canvas

Art on canvas usually refers to an oil or acrylic painting; however, photographic images can also be printed onto canvas. In recent years it has become fashionable to display art on canvas without a frame. The image is printed with extended borders that "wraparound" the edges of the stretcher, producing an effect that means the image will not necessarily require a frame. However, a frame can easily be added in the future if you think it would improve the image, or if fashions change.

Stretcher bars

Canvas stretcher bars are purpose-made to standard sizes. They are readily available from most art supply stores and come in sizes from 4–30 inches (100–750mm) in 2 inch (50mm) increments. They are also available in larger sizes in larger increments up to 48 inches (1200mm). They are designed to interlock at the corners to form a "stretcher frame," and they are supplied with eight wooden wedges that fit into the inside corners to add a final stretch to the canvas.

If you have a nonstandard size canvas you may be able to choose a smaller size stretcher bar if you can position the canvas so that you do not cover any important parts of the image. Alternatively, you can make your own stretcher bars from 2 x 1–inch (50 x 25mm) batten. This can be mitered and joined in the same way as a normal frame to create any size stretcher that you require. However, you will not have the use of the wedges at the end of the process to add that final stretch to the canvas.

Ready-made stretcher bars

Wall stapler

Wooden mallet

Stretcher wedges

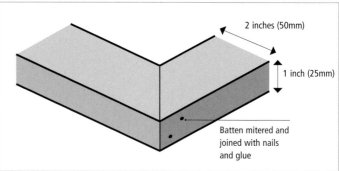

2 inches (50mm)

1 inch (25mm)

Batten mitered and joined with nails and glue

Handmade stretcher

Stretching a "wraparound" canvas

Tools and Materials

- STEEL RULER
- CANVAS STRETCHER BARS WITH WOODEN WEDGES
- WOODEN MALLET
- EMERY BOARD
- WALL STAPLER
- UTILITY KNIFE OR CRAFT KNIFE
- CANVAS STRETCHING PLIERS (OPTIONAL)
- TACK HAMMER
- MASKING TAPE (OPTIONAL)
- HANGINGS (SUCH AS D RING)
- TRI-SQUARE

Tip

Sometimes canvas stretcher bars have a sanded-down inner edge, but this may only be on one side. This is to stop a solid line forming on the canvas where the stretcher bar touches the back of the canvas. If your stretcher bars have this feature, make sure to keep all the smooth edges on one side of the stretcher when assembling. Also, remember to position the smooth edge next to the canvas when stretching it.

1 Measure the canvas picture to be stretched. For this example, the image measures 18 x 14 inches (450 x 350mm) and stretcher bars are usually ¾ inch (20mm) thick, so 16 x 12–inch (400 x 300mm) bars are used to allow the image to wrap around the edges of the stretcher.

2 Using four purpose-made stretcher bars—two measuring 16 inches (400mm) and two measuring 12 inches (300mm)—assemble the stretcher bars to form a rectangle. Use a wooden mallet to hammer the pieces together if necessary.

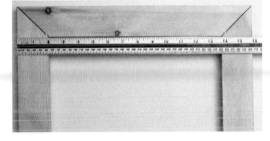

3 Measure across the stretcher bars to check for the correct size. This needs to be repeated at each edge of the rectangle to ensure the whole stretcher is evenly proportioned.

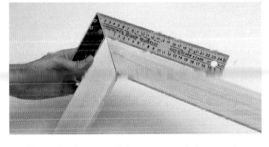

4 Check to see if the corners of the stretcher bars are at right angles and adjust as necessary. It is essential to get the stretcher frame square because it will show when hung if it is not. (Also, if you are going to frame the canvas it may not fit into the frame if it is crooked.)

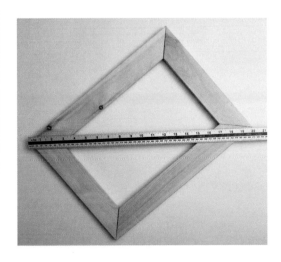

5 To make absolutely sure the stretcher frame is completely square, measure the diagonals of the stretcher frame. If they are the same measurement, the stretcher frame is square.

6 Any sharp corners of the stretcher may cut through the canvas over time, so be sure to sand them down with an emery board.

7 Position the canvas onto the stretcher frame. Be sure to position the picture so that no white unfinished canvas will show after stretching. Also, take care to leave the artist's signature (if present) showing.

8 Once you are happy with the positioning of the canvas, turn it over so that you can work from the back. Keeping everything in the desired position, pull one of the excesses of canvas down onto the back of the stretcher frame.

9 Using a wall stapler, secure the canvas in the center of one of the long sides with one staple. It is a good idea to use the staple gun at a diagonal angle so that the staples are not positioned entirely along one weave of the canvas because the multiple holes can fray and eventually tear the canvas. Make sure you staple on the back of the canvas and not on the side, where it will be visible.

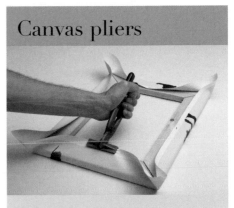

Canvas pliers

You can also use canvas-stretching pliers. These make a more even stretch on bigger canvases a lot easier to achieve. They are not an essential tool, but they can be useful if canvas stretching becomes a regular picture-framing project for you.

10 Turn the canvas around so that you can pull against the first staple. Pull firmly to apply stretch to the canvas and then secure in place with another staple.

11 If there is an excessive amount of canvas it will get in the way and also make a neat fold at the corners difficult to achieve, so remove some of the excess canvas with scissors but be sure to leave enough to easily grab hold of. Repeat steps 9 and 10 for the remaining two sides of the canvas.

12 Continue stretching the canvas, adding one staple at a time. Add stretch to the canvas, staple it in place, and then pull on the opposite side. You should always be pulling against the last staple you added.

13 The corners will need to look neat from the sides, and the folds should only be visible from the top and bottom. The technique is exactly the same as making a bed with a flat undersheet. First, choose a corner and pull the canvas from one of the side edges toward its opposite. A staple here will help to keep it in position.

14 Fold the top corner of the canvas underneath itself so it is hidden from view.

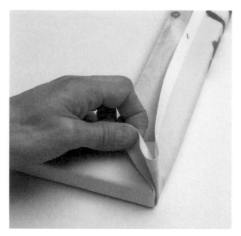

15 Fold the now double-thick remaining loose canvas over and secure it with a staple on top.

16 Repeat this process for the diagonally opposite corner. Remember to add stretch to the canvas by pulling it as you fold. Secure this corner with a staple as before.

17 Repeat for the remaining two corners. All of the corners should look neatly folded and the canvas should be fairly flat along the edges by the corners.

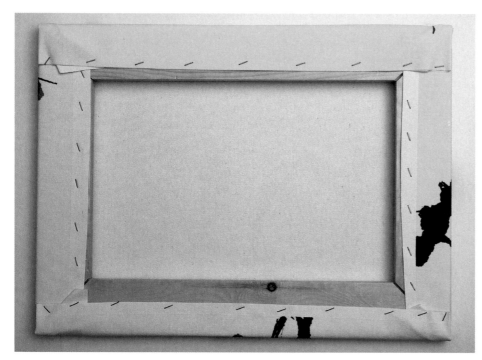

18 You may need to add additional staples toward the corners of the canvas to achieve an even stretch to the picture.

19 To add a final stretch, carefully insert the wooden stretcher wedges into the gaps in the corners of the stretcher bars.

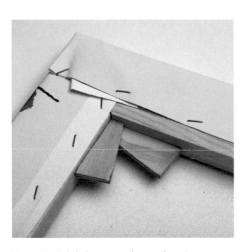

20 Lightly hammer the wedges home with a tack hammer. Be very careful not to hammer them too far because too much stretch could rip the canvas. The tension should allow some movement in the canvas when pushed in the middle of the picture. It should not be as tight as a drum.

21 To tidy up the back of the canvas, gummed paper tape may be added to cover the staples. However, this is not essential.

22 Add a suitable hanger. A D ring screwed into the stretcher frame is a good idea as it helps to keep the canvas as flat as possible on the wall.

The unframed canvas is now ready to hang on the wall.

Stretching a canvas to be framed

If you're stretching a canvas that's to be framed, the frame will cover the unfinished canvas on the edge of the frame. Therefore, positioning onto the stretcher frame needs to be very accurate. Also, make sure that you don't cover the artist's signature with the frame rabbet.

Sometimes artists sign pictures very near to the edge of the image so you may need to position the canvas slightly higher on the stretcher frame.

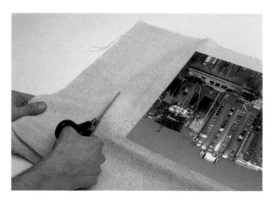

1 The techniques for stretching a canvas to be framed are almost identical as for the wraparound canvas, with a couple of key exceptions.

2 Assemble the stretcher bars as you did for the wraparound canvas on page 107.

4 If you are using canvas-stretching pliers, make sure you remove any excessive amount of canvas at the edges so you can achieve a good grip with the pliers. Be careful not to cut off too much canvas though.

5 Staples can be fired into the side of the stretcher frame. This can be easier than firing into the back of the frame, especially if you don't have a large excess of canvas.

6 The corners of the canvas are stretched in exactly the same way as for the wraparound canvas (see page 110). Special care should be taken here to get the corners as flat as possible as these will form the widest width of the finished stretched canvas. If they protrude too much the canvas may not fit into the frame.

7 Extra security can be added by also stapling into the back of the frame. This could be used to add extra stretch to any uneven areas.

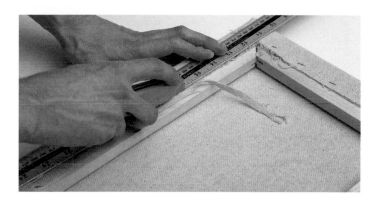

Tip

Art on canvas does not usually require glass because it is often an oil painting that will have been varnished to protect the surface. If you have a photograph printed on canvas you may need to add a varnish to protect it. Be sure to use a water-based varnish and sponge it onto the printed surface; don't use a brush because you may smudge the inks used to print your image.

8 Once stapled, any excess canvas can be trimmed off with a ruler and knife to neaten the finished effect.

Using off-set clips

1 Works of art on canvas do not need a deep "box" molding to frame them. By using off-set clips the canvas stretcher bars can be nailed in position.

2 First, nail the off-set clips into the rabbet of the frame. Be sure to bend them slightly back out of the way to allow the canvas to fit into the frame.

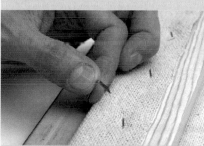

3 Place the canvas into the frame and nail the off-set clips into the back of the canvas stretcher to secure it to the frame.

The stretched canvas is now ready to frame.

chapter 5

Mat and frame decoration

Once you've mastered the techniques needed to create mats and frames you can explore mat and frame decoration. Mats can be decorated with pen lines, indented lines, colored bevels, and watercolor washes, and frames can be painted or given hand finishes, such as wax to enhance the natural grain of the wood. Mat and frame decoration can be used to emphasize key areas of the picture to be framed and can create very individual picture framing.

See also
Aesthetic decisions: *page 28*
Mat cutting: *page 38*

Mat decoration

The purpose of mat decoration is to emphasize key areas of a picture with the careful choice of colored lines. The combinations include single lines, multiple lines with an added wash band, colored bevels, and indented mats. Mat decoration is added using a variety of techniques, which use both watercolor and pens.

To add lines correctly to overmats it is necessary to know where to start and stop each line. The start and stop points are made with either a pencil or a pin, depending on the style of line. A template needs to be constructed before the mat can be decorated.

The mat for this watercolor painting has line and wash decoration.

Tools and Materials

- THIN CARDSTOCK
- STRAIGHT EDGE
- RULER
- PENCIL
- SELF-HEALING CUTTING MAT
- KNIFE
- ADHESIVE PUTTY
- MAT CUTTER

1 Using the thin piece of cardstock mark out a piece 12 x 12 inches (300 x 300mm).

Tip

The border of the mat needs to be wide enough to accommodate your mat decoration. It is best to cut a wider border than you think you will need, then cut down the mat-border after decoration to avoid the decoration dominating the picture. It is easy to go over the top with mat decoration so do keep this in mind. Also, remember that subtle mat decoration using watercolors will only be visible on lighter-colored matboards.

Tip

It is best not to use thick matboard for the mat decoration templates because the thickness can cause inaccuracies in marking out due to parallax. The pencil or pin may be aligned with the top surface of the matboard but, by the time the marker reaches the overmat, inaccuracies can occur.

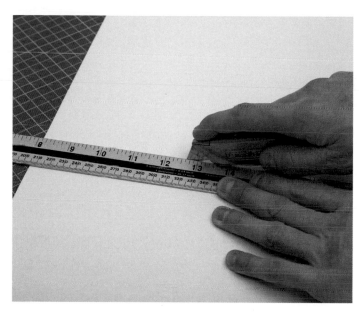

2 Using the ruler and knife, cut out the piece of cardstock you have marked up. Remember to secure the ruler in place using adhesive putty before cutting.

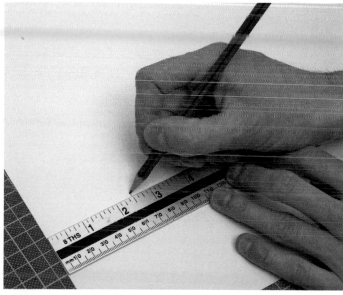

3 Mark out a 2½-inch (62mm) border all around the piece of cardstock.

The template

The cardstock should look like this when correctly marked out.

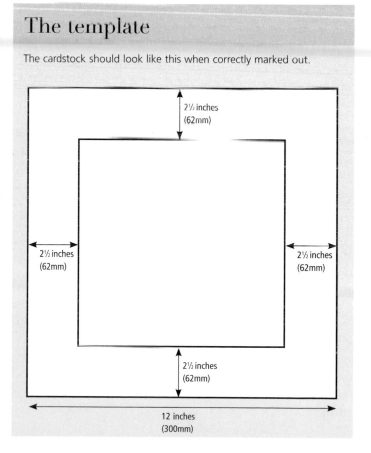

2½ inches (62mm)

2½ inches (62mm)

2½ inches (62mm)

2½ inches (62mm)

12 inches (300mm)

4 Using the mat cutter, cut out the window of the thin cardstock as you would for a mat aperture.

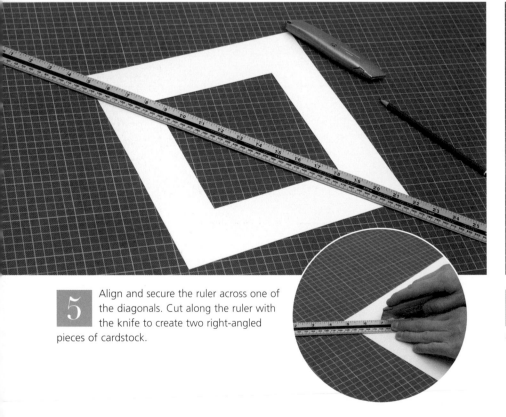

5 Align and secure the ruler across one of the diagonals. Cut along the ruler with the knife to create two right-angled pieces of cardstock.

6 Secure the ruler along the remaining diagonals of each piece of cardstock one at a time. This should produce four pieces of cardstock in the shape of a parallelogram.

7 Finally, cut each parallelogram in half to produce eight templates, enough for eight different mat decoration styles.

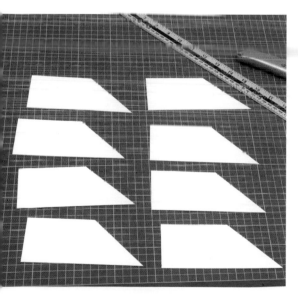

8 You can now begin to design your own mat decoration designs using the templates to mark up accurately the distances of the lines from the mat aperture.

Mat decoration designs

Mat decoration is a chance to make your picture framing unique. It is sensible to experiment with different line designs to discover which you think looks best. Below are some suggestions for line decoration. The designs can be anything that is deemed suitable; this is a really good opportunity to get creative. Try drawing some lines with a pencil on a piece of paper or a scrap of matboard and see if a random design will suit your picture.

A single mat with just one line can really enhance a picture.

A single mat with two lines can emphasize a specific area. The two lines could be different colors.

A single mat with three lines. Notice here the second and third lines are nearer to each other than the first and second. The first two lines could be the same color or all the lines could be the same color. The wider gap between the first two lines could be filled in with a watercolor wash band of color. (See "Watercolor decoration" page 126.)

See also
Mat decoration: *page 116*

Line decoration

Drawing just one line on an overmat is by far the most common technique used in mat decoration. It is often a single gold or silver line. The gold and silver lines are made using gold and silver pens. If you are only going to use one line, as a general rule the line should be at least ½ inch (10mm) away from the inner beveled edge of the mat.

This black and white photograph of a cat with a black mat is the sort of image which might be decorated with a single pen line.

Tools and Materials

- **MAT DECORATION TEMPLATE**
- **PENCIL**
- **RULER**
- **STRAIGHT EDGE**
- **MAT CUTTER RULER**
- **MAT TO BE DECORATED**
- **SEWING PIN**
- **SILVER OR GOLD PEN**

1 Using one of the mat decoration templates you have already (see page 116), make two pencil marks ½ inch (12mm) away from the top edge of the template.

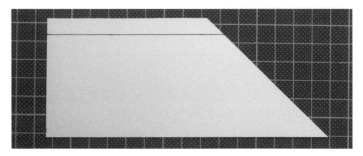

2 Join up these two marks to form a single pencil line on the template. The point where the pencil line meets the 45-degree angle on the template will be the start and stop points for each line. The lines should be at least ½ inch (12mm) away from the edge of the mat. Any less than this distance and any errors in the line become very obvious.

3 Position the template so that its top lines up with the edge of the bevel on the overmat, and so that the 45-degree edge of the template is aligned with the corner of the bevel on the mat.

4 Once the template is correctly positioned, use a pin to make a small hole in the matboard. Repeat steps 3 and 4 for the three remaining corners of the mat.

5 Position the ruler so that the start and stop points are clearly visible. The start/stop points should be used as a guide but the most important thing is to make sure the ruler is parallel with the edge of the mat. If the line is not parallel it will be immediately obvious to the viewer. Make a note of the measurement on the ruler where the stop point appears. The pin holes can be difficult to see, so a number predetermined on the ruler will ensure accuracy and reduce the risk of overshooting with the pen.

Draw the line along the ruler with the pen, remembering to stop at the stop point. A mental rehearsal of drawing the line before you begin may help. Gold and silver pens can often have an uneven flow of ink during use; if this happens the line can be drawn over again to cover any gaps. Before going over the line a second time check the flow of the ink on the scrap of cardstock.

Test the pen

Before using pens for line decoration, it's a good idea to shake them to ensure the ink will flow evenly. Test the pen on a scrap of matboard to be sure it's working.

Tip

The ruler that is used for the lines must be slightly raised away from the matboard at the edge of the ruler. Most rulers included with mat cutters have this little step feature built in. This is to make sure the ink from the pen's nib does not touch the edge of the ruler and then smudge as the ruler is lifted away. If your ruler does not have this feature, simply attach a strip of matboard along one side of the ruler with the edge of the matboard slightly in from the edge of the ruler. This will create the necessary elevation away from the matboard and keep the pen's nib away from the ruler.

Repeat step 5 for the three remaining lines. The resulting mat has a simple, single silver line.

Coloring the bevel

Bevels can be colored to further emphasize the three-dimensionality created by overmats. One of the most effective ways to use this technique is to color a white bevel on a white mat black to create the maximum contrast. But any color mat can have any color bevel added. Try a color combination of your choice on a scrap piece of matboard before the finished overmat is decorated, to see if it suits the picture.

White overmat on a black and white photograph.

Tools and Materials

- **THICK-NIBBED BLACK PEN**
- **WHITE OVERMAT**
- **THIN-NIBBED BLACK PEN**
- **RULER**

1 Using the thick-nibbed pen, test it on a scrap of matboard for consistency. Then, working from underneath, color in the bevel, working from one end to the other on each side. Do not try to go right into the corners as these will be touched in with the fine pen.

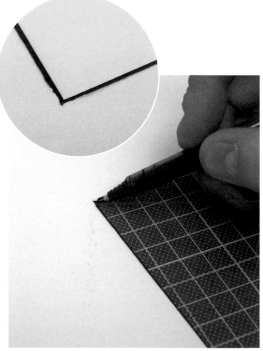

2 With care, use the thin-nibbed pen to fill in the corners of the bevel. The edge of the bevel may well appear uneven at this stage.

3 The uneven edge can be rectified by adding another line right on the very edge of the bevel. Align the ruler on the edge of the bevel, making sure you cover the uneven edge and draw along the ruler.

The bevel should now be evenly colored.

Different looks

Different looks can easily be created on the same photograph by simply adding a pen line, coloring a bevel, or by changing the color of the mat. This selection shows the subtle differences that can achieved.

Plain black mat.

Plain white mat.

To add emphasis to the mat decoration and contrast to the picture, a single black line could also be added on to the white mat with the black bevel.

Plain black mat with silver pen line.

Plain white mat with black-colored bevel.

See also
Mat decoration: *page 116*

Indenting overmats

Grooved lines can be indented into the surface of the overmat. This has the effect of creating a "plate line" impression, something that older-style printing incorporated. In this example a color photograph of a sailing scene is used with a cream-colored overmat.

Cream overmat on a color photograph.

An indenting tool can be any tool with a rounded, hard point. A bradawl is ideal for the job.

Other alternatives are a pair of scissors, a large paper clip, or any smooth, clean, rounded steel tool. Try experimenting with different tools to see the effect. Each line will probably need three sweeps with the tool to make each indented line clearly visible. Keep experimenting until you are confident you know what you are doing.

Bradawl

Tools and Materials

- **MAT DECORATION TEMPLATE**
- **PENCIL**
- **RULER**
- **INDENTING TOOL (OR BRADAWL)**
- **ADHESIVE PUTTY**
- **ERASER**

1 Mark out a single line on a mat-decorating template ½ inch (12mm) from the top of the edge of the template.

2 Using a pencil mark out the start/stop points on the mat. The pencil marks can easily be erased when the indented line is completed.

3 Align the ruler with the start and stop points. Make a mental note of the measurement at which the stop point lines up with the ruler; this will assist accuracy and help to avoid overshooting. When the ruler is aligned, run the indenting tool along the ruler three times to make the line clearly visible. Make sure your indenting tool is thoroughly clean before you start.

Repeat step 3 for the remaining three sides to complete the indented line.

Watercolor decoration

Watercolor paints are used for a traditional form of mat decoration called line and wash. Line and wash is used to form a combination of colored lines and bands (washes) on overmats. The example shown here is a watercolor seascape of Anglesey, Wales, with a cream mat used to complement the delicate lines.

Watercolor painting with a cream mat.

The lines on a wash line mat are created using ruling pens. They are filled by being dipped into reservoirs of watercolor. The pens need to be pressed quite firmly onto the matboard to create each line. Practice drawing wash lines on scraps of matboard before decorating the finished mat.

Wash bands are created with watercolor brushes. It is a good idea to have a variety of watercolor brushes for different widths of wash bands. Wash lines do not have to be used in conjunction with wash bands; one or two colored lines alone can be very effective using watercolor and ruling pens.

Watercolor paint is available in several different types. Tubes of color tend to be more expensive but a good consistency of color is more likely. A palette of block colors is a good idea as color mixing is made far easier.

A palette to mix each color is needed but a cheap substitute is a 6- or 12-cup muffin pan. As long as each cup is deep enough to dip the ruling pen into, a muffin pan will work very well.

Tools and Materials

- **MAT-DECORATION TEMPLATE**
- **PENCIL**
- **RULER**
- **WATERCOLOR PAINTS (TUBES OR PANS)**
- **PALETTE**
- **RULING PEN**
- **PAPER TOWEL**
- **PAINTBRUSHES**
- **ERASER**

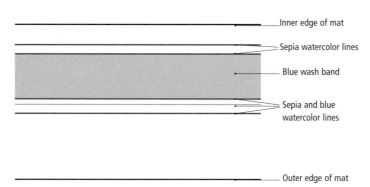

Inner edge of mat

Sepia watercolor lines

Blue wash band

Sepia and blue watercolor lines

Outer edge of mat

1 The first stage is to decide on the design combination of wash and lines. For this example, a combination of five lines with a wash band between the second and third lines has been chosen. The first, second, third, and fifth lines are a sepia to match the rock of the shoreline in the picture. The fourth line and the wash band are blue to match the color of the sea.

2 Using a pencil and ruler, mark up your design of watercolor lines and wash band onto a mat decoration template.

3 Mark out the overmat using the template and a pencil. The pencil marks can be erased when the watercolor is completely dry.

4 Using water and a fine paintbrush, mix your chosen colors in the palette.

Tip

If you are a watercolor artist, line-and-wash decoration may really appeal to you because the colors used in each of your watercolors can easily be replicated to emphasize your favorite areas of each picture.

5 Practice loading the ruling pen with watercolor by dipping it into the palette. Remove the excess paint from the outside edges of the ruling pen with a piece of paper towel.

6 Test the consistency of the watercolor on a scrap of matboard before you begin. Allow the watercolor line to dry and see what the line color/strength/width looks like with the picture. Adjust the watercolor mixture or line width to suit.

Tubes of watercolor paint

Ruling pen

Watercolor brushes

Palette of pan colors

Mixing palette

Watercolor brushes

When choosing the wash/line combination, try to match up the wash band width with the width of the brushes available. This will make the wash band easier to achieve.

7 Once you have the color and consistency of the paint as you want it, draw the first line on the mat. As always, use the measurements along the ruler, as well as the pencil marks, to help you to remember exactly where to start and stop.

8 Turn the overmat 90 degrees and draw the second side of the first line. Then continue in this way, finally joining the fourth side with the first.

9 Repeat steps 6 and 7 for the remaining lines, remembering to change colors as needed for the desired effect. Allow the lines to dry. This will take at least 10 minutes, depending on ambient temperature.

10 Mix the color you want for the wash band. This should be a lot lighter than the lines, so a lot less pigment will be needed. Again, test for consistency on a scrap of matboard and allow the tester to dry before continuing.

11 Once the correct color has been mixed, apply water to one corner of the overmat using the chosen width of brush. This will form the start/stop point of the watercolor wash band. Ideally, the watercolor should not be totally dry as you finish the band, so use a reasonable amount of water and, this will enable you to blend the start and stop points of the band, giving a seamless finish.

12 As you apply the wash, move the mat around 90 degrees at time. Try to keep an even flow of watercolor from the brush, so keep dipping it into the palette regularly. A second sweep will help to even out the paint and create a smooth wash band. Keep a piece of paper towel close to hand, so that any mistakes can be quickly swabbed off and will not show when dry.

Once the watercolor wash is dry the overmat is ready to attach to the picture.

Applying wax to frames

To enhance frames successfully it is usually best to use plain wood frames. These are easier to decorate because they do not have any finishes on them, such as varnish, that prevent stains, paints, and waxes from sinking into the wood. The technique shown in this section involves waxes.

Plain wood frame

Paint

Waxes

Sandpaper

Paintbrushes

Steel wool

Tools and Materials

- **LIMING WAX**
- **PLAIN WOODEN FRAME**
- **FINE SANDPAPER**
- **STEEL WOOL (FOR FINER FINISHES)**
- **CRAFT GLUE**
- **PAPER TOWEL**
- **DISPOSABLE GLOVES**
- **COTTON CLOTH**

To decorate plain wood frames, the picture framer can use waxes, paints, or stains. This section covers wax, but the techniques are very similar for all of these media.

Waxes are available in many different tones and the application of a natural or clear wax to a frame will tend to exaggerate the effect of the grain. Therefore the more open grain may well be enhanced further on harder woods such as ash or oak. The effects may not be so noticeable, or create so much contrast on pine or softer obeche woods, and it is recommended that each wax is tried on an offcut to check for suitability and general effect before you use it on a full frame. In this demonstration liming wax is going to be applied to plain ash molding. The effect is purposefully uneven with some areas of plain wood showing through.

Tip

There are many unusual wood finishes available on the market. Home improvement television programs have made these ideas fashionable and a trip to the local DIY or paint suppliers will yield many unusual styles of wood stains. Why not try a small mixer tin on a scrap of molding to see what can be created?

1 After selecting your preferred wax (liming wax in this case), rub down the frame with fine sandpaper. Pay particular attention to any rough areas.

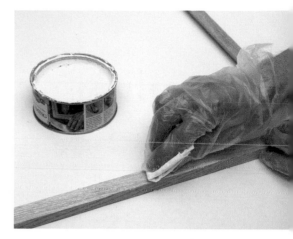

2 If there are any gaps in the miters of the frame, apply some craft glue to the gap and remove any excess glue with a piece of paper towel.

3 Sand again, making sure to move the sandings into the glue in the corners. These will act as an excellent filler for any corners that are not quite perfect. Any sawdust from the miter saw can also be sprinkled into the glue before finishing off with the sandpaper.

4 Using protective disposable gloves apply the wax with a cotton cloth. Make sure you rub plenty of wax into the frame, working with the grain, and do not forget to cover all visible surfaces, for example along the rabbet. Buff the frame with a clean cloth to remove any excess wax.

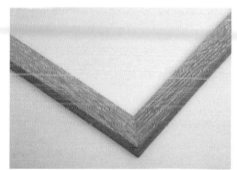

5 Allow the wax to dry.

Once the wax has dried, fit the picture into the frame. The limed wax effect is in keeping with this monochrome charcoal drawing of a horse.

Painting a picture frame

An incredible range of pre-decorated frames is available but many people still prefer hand-painted frames, with colors and finishes chosen specifically for the picture. The techniques shown here utilize water-based paints. They are user-friendly, the brushes are easy to clean, and they tend to have far less odor than oil-based paints.

This black and white photograph of a cat has a plain wooden frame. A black-painted frame might better complement this image.

Tools and Materials

- PLAIN WOODEN FRAME
- FINE SANDPAPER
- CRAFT GLUE
- PREMIXED FILLER
- FILLER KNIFE
- BLACK LATEX PAINT
- PAINTBRUSH
- STEEL WOOL (OPTIONAL)
- DISPOSABLE GLOVES
- CLEAR WAX
- COTTON CLOTH

1 Assemble the plain wood frame as usual.

3 Fill in any gaps in the corners with the combination of craft glue and sandings.

2 Smooth down the frame with sandpaper with particular attention to any rough areas.

4 Any dents or large gaps can be filled using premixed filler and a filler knife. Once the filler has dried, smooth down any rough areas with sandpaper. As the frame is going to be painted, the filler will not show when the frame is finished.

5 Once the filler or glue has dried and the frame has been smoothed down with sandpaper, apply the first coat of paint and allow to dry.

6 When the frame is dry, rub down the first coat of paint with steel wool or fine sandpaper and apply a second coat of paint. Take particular care in the corners and paint with the grain of the wood. Do not overload the brush with paint as the brush strokes will show. Apply as many coats as needed to cover the frame entirely; the frame will probably need at least three coats for an even color.

7 Water-based paints need to be sealed with a wax or varnish. The best material to use is a clear wax. Using protective disposable gloves, apply the wax with a cotton cloth and then buff off.

When the wax is dry (after several minutes) the picture can be fitted into the frame. Here, the white mat has also been decorated with a single black line and a colored bevel.

See also
Frame decoration: *page 130*
Painting a picture frame: *page 132*

Gilding

Traditional, high-quality gilded finishes are difficult to achieve and, ideally, you would ask an experienced gilder to apply them for you. However, there are alternatives well worth trying: Transfer gilding does not provide such an effective gilded finish as traditional water gilding but is less expensive, simpler, and quicker to apply.

Transfer gilding

Gilding is a form of frame decoration that is traditionally done with gold leaf, but gold colors are also made from a mixture of other metals, mainly brass and copper. These imitation golds are available as fine powders, thin metal leaf, or gold paint and wax. They are more often used than genuine gold leaf because they are much cheaper and easier to apply.

The leaf sold for transfer gilding is backed with paper but you can also use loose leaf.

The traditional glue is called oil gold size but recently a water-soluble glue has been developed, which is easier to use and more flexible in terms of drying time.

Whether you are using real gold leaf or one of the many imitations, it is necessary to have a smooth, even surface to work on. All gilded finishes are reflective and will show up any flaws in the surface of the frame very clearly. So give your frame an undercoat of paint before gilding.

Tools and Materials

- **WOODEN FRAME WITH UNDERCOAT APPLIED**
- **PAINTBRUSH**
- **WATER-BASED GOLD SIZE**
- **TRANSFER GOLD LEAF (REAL OR IMITATION)**

Using gold leaf

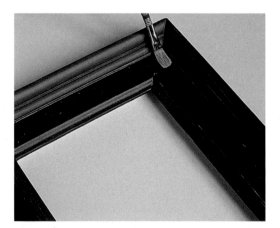

1 A coat of water-based gold size should be painted over the undercoat. The gold size is the glue that will adhere the transfer gold leaf to the frame, so it needs to be applied evenly, if that doesn't happen, the thinner areas will be ready for gilding before the rest.

2 After about 15 minutes the size is dry enough to start laying the leaf. Transfer leaf is loose gold that has been pressed onto transparent paper, which makes it easier to apply. Take the leaf and press it onto the frame, gold side down, applying even pressure with your finger.

Using imitation gold

1   Imitation gold leaf is loose rather than paper-backed leaf. It can be cut into the appropriate sizes with a craft knife.

2   Unlike genuine gold or silver leaf, imitation leaf can be picked up with fingers and placed into position, or thin cardboard can be folded and used as tweezers to pick it up.

3   To press the leaf firmly over the underlying ornament, tissue or thin plastic can be used as a barrier so that no glue is transferred to the fingers. This makes it easier to stick the gold closely to the surface of the frame. Imitation gold and silver leaf need to be protected form tarnishing by applying coats of shellac or specialist lacquer.

COMMERCIAL MOLDINGS
A wide variety of ready-made gilded moldings are available from framing suppliers. (See page 20.)

Resources

In this section advice is given on where to obtain tools, materials, and advice on all aspects of picture framing, as well as some useful contact details.

TOOLS AND EQUIPMENT

The Framing Teacher web site is a good resource for buying framing tools. The site is written and updated by the author. Tools can be bought in kits or individually. www.framingteacher.co.uk

Amazon is a useful resource for all tools, both new and second-hand; it is especially useful for miter saws/miter boxes. www.amazon.com

eBay is a global marketplace for both new and second-hand tools and equipment at reasonable prices. Be sure to check each seller's feedback and also check delivery charges and conditions. www.ebay.com

Saws and vises should be available at most hardware stores, especially the larger outlets. Call first to check whether the item that you require is in stock.

MATERIALS

Materials are available from the same sources listed for tools and equipment. However, it is best to visit a local art or picture framing store for the largest possible range. Take along the pictures to be framed so that the colors and styles of matboards and frames can be selected to complement each picture. Most professional picture framers should supply the moldings by the length or even as mitered sticks. However, some picture framers are reluctant to supply these materials to the amateur because they want you to use them, but be persistent.

GLASS

Glass should be cut by a professional glazier or picture framer. Take the finished picture frame along with you to ensure that the glass will definitely fit. Most glaziers will stock $\frac{1}{16}$–inch (2mm) picture framing glass but check before visiting.

ADVICE

The author is contactable through both of his web sites at www.framingteacher.co.uk and www.petersfieldframing.co.uk and will be glad to answer any questions that may arise about picture framing.

The Framer's Forum is an online picture-framing forum that tends to attract a professional following but the amateur market is well catered for. It is a very friendly forum and has always been very useful in times of need for the author. Visit theframersforum.com for further advice.

CONTACTS

Suppliers of framing materials and tools.

American Frame Corporation
400 Tomahawk Drive
Maumee, Ohio 43537
1-888-628-3833
www.americanframe.com

Art Materials Service, Inc.
625 Joyce Kilmer Avenue
New Brunswick
NJ 08901 USA
732-545-8888
www.artmaterialsservice.com

Artist and Display Supply
9015 West Burleigh Street
Milwaukee, WI 53222-3631
1-800-722-7450
www.artistanddisplay.com

Daniel Smith
P.O. Box 84268
Seattle, WA 98124-5568
(800) 426-6740
www.danielsmith.com

Blick Art Materials
P.O. Box 1267
Galesburg, IL 61402-1267
(800) 828-4548
www.dickblick.com

Frame Fit Company
P.O. Box 12727
Philadelphia
PA 19134
1-800-523-3693
www.framefit.com

Frames by Mail
11440 Schenk Drive
Maryland Heights
MO 63043
(800) 332-2467
www.framesbymail.com

Graphik Dimensions
2103 Brentwood Street
High Point, NC 27263 1807
(800) 221-0262
www.pictureframes.com

Jerry's Artarama
Order dept.
PO BOX 58638J
Raleigh, NC 27658-8638
1-800-827-8478
www.jerrysartarama.com

Light Impressions
PO Box 2100
Santa Fe Springs
CA 90670 800-828-6216
(800) 828-6216
www.lightimpressionsdirect.com

Miller's Art Supply
33332 W. 12 Milo Road,
Farmington Hills, MI 48334
248-489-8070
www.millersart.comm

Pearl Paints
308 Canal Street,
New York, NY 10013
212-431-7932
www.pearlpaint.com

Glossary

Acrylic
Tough and inflexible type of plastic that is sometimes used in framing instead of glass.

Backing board
This is the board that forms the back surface of the finished frame. It can be made from grayboard, millboard, medium-density fiberboard (MDF), hardboard, plyboard, or matboard.

Backing sheet
Backing sheet is used to create a layer of less acidic material between your picture and the backing board. This helps to protect your picture from impurities that may be in the poorer quality backing sheets.

Beading
Narrow strip of wood, often ornamental, sometimes used as an additional component of a frame.

Bevel
The sloping 45-degree edge on the inside window of a mat.

Box frame
Deep frames designed to display 3-D objects, such as medals, behind glass. Also used for needlework and sometimes for oil paintings with a particularly thick build-up of paint.

Box molding
Deep molding used to make box frames.

Clip frame
A simple frame without an edge or surround, formed by clipping a sheet of glass to a wooden backing.

Conservation matboard
High quality matboard which is "acid-free" or "neutral pH;" the lower levels of acid in the board will help to preserve your works of art.

D ring
Hanging fixture comprising a D-shaped ring and a screw plate. Flatter than screw rings.

Double mat
When two mats are used to border a picture to add depth or to bring out colors in the artwork.

Dry mounting
A method of sticking a picture onto a backing. A sheet of film is placed between the two and heat and/or pressure is applied. The film dissolves, fusing the picture and backing.

Emery
Stick or paper covered with emery powder, used for fine sanding.

Fillet
Thin strip of wood, or layered matboard, that fits under the rebate and is used to support the glass in a box frame. It is less deep than the frame molding to allow space for the picture and backing board.

Frame size
The dimensions of the frame which are always $\frac{1}{16}$ inch (2mm) bigger than the "outside size."

Gilding
Applying a gold finish.

Glass plate
Primarily used for mirrors, glass plates are screwed to both the frame and the wall and are visible once the piece is hung. They can also be used for heavier frames.

Inside size
The measurement taken from the inside of the mat.

Lacing
A piece of needlework can be stretched across a board by lacing the fabric with thread across the back.

Mat
The card surround used to protect and display a work. Mats are usually cut with an aperture behind which the picture fits, and the inner edges are beveled.

Mat cutter
Device for cutting neat and accurate bevels into matboard.

Miter
The 45-degree angled cut made in each end of a piece of frame molding so that they meet at a 90-degree angle (miter joint).

Miter saw
A saw designed specifically for cutting miters. The blade is held in place by two steel columns mounted on a metal base.

Miter vise
A right-angled vise, designed to join two pieces of mitered molding together at 90 degrees.

Molding
A shaped length of wood. Picture frame moldings have a rebate behind which the picture fits (and the mat and glass if used). Carpenter's moldings, used for baseboards, trimmings around doors, etc., have no rebate, but can sometimes be adapted for frame making.

Multiple aperture mats
Mats with more than one aperture cut into them in order to display multiple images.

Outside size
The measurement taken from the outer edge of the mat/glass/backing "sandwich."

Profile
The word used to describe the shape of a molding.

Rabbet
The L-shaped groove on the inside edge of picture frame molding into which the picture, glass, mat, and backing board fit.

Reverse molding
A molding which has the highest part next to the picture and slopes away at the outer edge.

Sampler
Piece of needlework that traditionally has a border incorporated into the design.

"Sandwich"
The artwork, overmat, backing and barrier board, and the glass, when secured together prior to insertion into the frame are referred to as the picture framing "sandwich."

Score
Cutting a line in glass or card that does not pass completely through the material in order to aid precise folding or breaking.

Screw rings
Simple hanging fixings, which are screwed into the back of the frame; picture cord or wire is threaded through them.

Slip frame
An inner frame, often covered in fabric, inserted between the main frame and picture to provide a decorative border.

Slip mat see double mat

Stretcher
A wooden frame over which canvas is stretched.

Transfer gold or silver
Thin sheets of beaten gold or silver, attached to paper and rubbed onto the surface of a frame.

Wash line
A form of decoration used on mats, usually for watercolors. A pale wash of watercolor is painted around the whole mat a small distance from the aperture, and finished with fine pen lines.

Wet mounting
A method of sticking a picture to a backing, using glue.

Window
The aperture cut into a mat through which the picture is viewed.

Wraparound effect
A canvas stretched so that the picture continues onto the edges of the stretcher, remaining visible on the sides. The canvas is then tacked/stapled on the back of the stretchers so that the canvas requires no frame. The corners of the canvas are neatly folded.

Index

Credits

Quarto would like to thank the following artists and agencies for kindly supplying images for inclusion in this book.

Corbis: pages 4, 21, 72, 73, 74

Gordon Rushmer: page 116
www.gordonrushmer.co.uk

Ann Hollaway: page 28
www.darkeye.org.uk

Naomi Sheed: page 25
www.naomisheed.com

Shutterstock

Jackie Walker: page 30
www.hazymoonstudio.com